A Donation has been made to the
Clay County Public Library
In Memory Of:

Leonard Donaldson

This Donation has been made by:

Billie & Bobby Stone

1st EDITION

Perspectives on Modern World History

The Persian Gulf War

1st EDITION

Perspectives on Modern World History

The Persian Gulf War

Alexander Cruden

Book Editor

GREENHAVEN PRESS
A part of Gale, Cengage Learning

GALE
CENGAGE Learning

Detroit • New York • San Francisco • New Haven, Conn • Waterville, Maine • London

Christine Nasso, *Publisher*
Elizabeth Des Chenes, *Managing Editor*

© 2011 Greenhaven Press, a part of Gale, Cengage Learning.

Gale and Greenhaven Press are registered trademarks used herein under license.

For more information, contact:
Greenhaven Press
27500 Drake Rd.
Farmington Hills, MI 48331-3535
Or you can visit our Internet site at gale.cengage.com.

For product information and technology assistance, contact us at
Gale Customer Support, 1-800-877-4253.

For permission to use material from this text or product, submit all requests online at
www.cengage.com/permissions.

Further permissions questions can be e-mailed to permissionrequest@cengage.com.

Articles in Greenhaven Press anthologies are often edited for length to meet page requirements. In addition, original titles of these works are changed to clearly present the main thesis and to explicitly indicate the author's opinion. Every effort is made to ensure that Greenhaven Press accurately reflects the original intent of the authors. Every effort has been made to trace the owners of copyrighted material.

Cover image Custom Medical Stock Photo, Inc. Reproduced by permission.

LIBRARY OF CONGRESS CATALOGING-IN-PUBLICATION DATA

The Persian Gulf War / Alexander Cruden, book editor.
   p. cm. -- (Perspectives on modern world history)
   Includes bibliographical references and index.
  ISBN 978-0-7377-5261-8 (hardcover)
  1. Persian Gulf War, 1991--Juvenile literature. I. Cruden, Alex.
   DS79.723.P48 2011
   956.7044'2--dc22
                                              2010042766

Printed in the United States of America
1 2 3 4 5 6 7 15 14 13 12 11

CONTENTS

Foreword   1

Introduction   4

World Map   9

CHAPTER **1**   Historical Background on the
                Persian Gulf War

1. An Overview of the War and Its Causes   13
   Anthony H. Cordesman

   Set off by Iraq's invasion of Kuwait, the
   Persian Gulf War united several Arab nations
   with military forces led by the United States
   in an extraordinary coalition. The allies' superior airpower, technology, strategy, training,
   and coordination overwhelmed Iraqi
   troops.

2. How Saddam Hussein Prepared for
   the War   28
   Lawrence Freedman and Efraim Karsh

   Rather than lose status by pulling back from
   Kuwait under international diplomatic pressure, Iraq's leader decided to risk war with
   the United States. He figured that Americans
   would be reluctant to fight and accept the
   casualties of military action.

3. The US President Takes Action to
   Oppose Iraq   42
   George H.W. Bush

In a then-secret document preceding
Operation Desert Storm, President George
H.W. Bush outlines US interests in the Persian
Gulf region and what the United States is
doing in response to Iraq's invasion of Kuwait.
The response includes deployment of US
forces to the area.

4. Baghdad Celebrates a New Year While
   on the Brink of War   49
   Elaine Sciolino

A *New York Times* foreign correspondent
living in Iraq's capital finds officials trying to
maintain normalcy while ordinary Iraqis are
either confident that military action will be
averted or assume a catastrophic conflict is
likely at any moment.

5. Why the United States Decided to
   Attack   60
   George H.W. Bush

Two hours after allied air attacks begin in Iraq
and Kuwait, the US president tells the public
why the war is taking place. He explains that
attacking was the only remaining way to coun-
ter the atrocities committed by and the dangers posed by Iraqi leader Saddam Hussein.

6. The Persian Gulf Region Was Highly
   Unstable and Militarized   68
   Abdulkhaleq Abdulla

Two of the main factors leading to Operation
Desert Storm were that the Persian Gulf
region had been historically and constantly
oriented toward conflict and that the area had
been dominated by foreign powers.

CHAPTER 2   Controversies Surrounding the Persian Gulf War

1. The War Was Absolutely Justifiable   **80**

   James Turner Johnson

   The decision to launch Operation Desert Storm was fully justified and met all criteria for a just war. The amount of force used was appropriate and the military action was motivated by the goal of making peace possible in the region.

2. The War Was an Unjustifiable Exercise of Arrogance   **92**

   Alan Geyer and Barbara G. Green

   It is dangerous and perverse to assume that the US-led military success makes the resort to war acceptable. Instead of whipping up a rush-to-war emotion, the allies should have persisted with economic sanctions against the Iraqi leadership.

3. Israel Played a Vital Role in Helping the US Effort   **99**

   Mitchell Bard

   The United States asked Israel not to participate in the war, even though Israel was attacked by Iraqi Scud missiles. Nevertheless, Israel was able to support the military effort in more than a dozen ways, and thus deter Arab extremism.

4. The United States Can Preserve a Structure for Mideast Peace   **109**

   William J. Perry

   The extraordinary military capability

demonstrated by the United States now should be used for deterrence, rather than more fighting. The US "force multipliers" are so strong that other countries should avoid starting regional warfare.

5. The Region's Power Structure Changed Considerably   **116**

Saul B. Cohen

Iraq's defeat left its neighbors safer, opened the door for Egypt to become more dominant, and moved resolution of the Arab-Israeli conflict closer. The war also demonstrated the establishment of the United States as a preeminent force in the Middle East.

6. Desert Storm Was a Criminal Assault on Defenseless People   **125**

Ramsey Clark

Children, elderly people, and other civilians died by the tens of thousands while US forces perpetuated a myth of precision military action. And after Desert Storm ended, the American-led embargo was in effect a genocidal policy.

7. Arab Leaders Could Have Prevented the War   **136**

Majid Khadduri and Edmund Ghareeb

A greater understanding of Islamic culture helps show that this war did not have to happen. An Arab summit just before Kuwait was invaded missed an opportunity to avert conflict. And the West—led by the United States—acted impatiently.

8. The War Sickened More Than One
Fourth of US Troops   143

*Research Advisory Committee on Gulf
War Veterans' Illnesses*

A federal study group concluded that the evidence strongly suggests that pills taken by US troops and pesticides unleashed during the war brought a complex of afflictions to more than 170,000 veterans.

9. The Bush Administration Kept the Public
from Learning the Whole Truth   151

Jacqueline Sharkley

The United States won big and handily in the fight with Iraq, right? That's the picture most Americans received—because the press was tightly restricted by the military. The Bush administration spun the images to its advantage.

CHAPTER 3   Personal Narratives

1. A US Army Officer Sees the First
Invaders Enter Kuwait City   165

Martin Stanton

While on a weekend break on his own in a hotel in Kuwait, a US major is awakened by gunfire. Looking out his window, he sees the first wave of Iraqi troops rolling into the capital—on what look like school buses.

2. The War Is Fragments of Bravery,
Death, and Confusion   175

Buzz Williams

A young Marine Corps reservist, rushed into combat, tells of the gritty existence and helter-skelter warfare in the desert—attacking Iraqis, dealing with split-second life-and-death ambiguity, and encountering children on the battlefield.

3. For Women in Combat, the Greatest Challenge Is Control   **183**

Rhonda Cornum, as told to Peter Copeland

Shot down while flying to the aid of an injured pilot, an American woman/Army major/medical doctor is injured and held captive. She tells how Operation Desert Storm changed her—and women in the military in general.

4. The Lives of Iraqi Teenagers Changed Drastically Because of the War   **194**

Nadje Al-Ali and Yasmin Hussein

After the war, a typical teenager's day was no longer predictable or even safe. Despite strong family ties, the main desire expressed by many Iraqi young people was to leave their homeland as soon as possible. Getting a good education remained a priority for some.

Chronology   **203**

For Further Reading   **206**

Index   **209**

FOREWORD

"History cannot give us a program for the future, but it can give us a fuller understanding of our-selves, and of our common humanity, so that we can better face the future."

—Robert Penn Warren,
American poet and novelist

The history of each nation is punctuated by momentous events that represent turning points for that nation, with an impact felt far beyond its borders. These events—displaying the full range of human capabilities, from violence, greed, and ignorance to heroism, courage, and strength—are nearly always complicated and multifaceted. Any student of history faces the challenge of grasping the many strands that constitute such world-changing events as wars, social movements, and environmental disasters. But understanding these significant historic events can be enhanced by exposure to a variety of perspectives, whether of people involved intimately or of ones observing from a distance of miles or years. Understanding can also be increased by learning about the controversies surrounding such events and exploring hot-button issues from multiple angles. Finally, true understanding of important historic events involves knowledge of the events' human impact—of the ways such events affected people in their everyday lives—all over the world.

Perspectives on Modern World History examines global historic events from the twentieth-century onward by presenting analysis and observation from numerous vantage points. Each volume offers high school, early college level, and general interest readers a thematically arranged anthology of previously published materials that address a major historical event, with an emphasis on international coverage. Each volume opens with background information on the event, then presents the controversies surrounding that event, and concludes with first-person narratives from people who lived through the event or were affected by it. By providing primary sources from the time of the event, as well as relevant commentary surrounding the event, this series can be used to inform debate, help develop critical thinking skills, increase global awareness, and enhance an understanding of international perspectives on history.

Material in each volume is selected from a diverse range of sources, including journals, magazines, newspapers, nonfiction books, personal narratives, speeches, congressional testimony, government documents, pamphlets, organization newsletters, and position papers. Articles taken from these sources are carefully edited and introduced to provide context and background. Each volume of Perspectives on Modern World History includes an array of views on events of global significance. Much of the material comes from international sources and from US sources that provide extensive international coverage.

Each volume in the Perspectives on Modern World History series also includes:

- A full-color **world map**, offering context and geographic perspective.
- An annotated **table of contents** that provides a brief summary of each essay in the volume.
- An **introduction** specific to the volume topic.
- For each viewpoint, a brief **introduction** that has notes about the author and source of the viewpoint, and that provides a summary of its main points.
- Full-color **charts**, **graphs**, **maps**, and other visual representations.

- Informational **sidebars** that explore the lives of key individuals, give background on historical events, or explain scientific or technical concepts.
- A **glossary** that defines key terms, as needed.
- A **chronology** of important dates preceding, during, and immediately following the event.
- A **bibliography** of additional books, periodicals, and Web sites for further research.
- A comprehensive **subject index** that offers access to people, places, and events cited in the text.

Perspectives on Modern World History is designed for a broad spectrum of readers who want to learn more about not only history but also current events, political science, government, international relations, and sociology—students doing research for class assignments or debates, teachers and faculty seeking to supplement course materials, and others wanting to improve their understanding of history. Each volume of Perspectives on Modern World History is designed to illuminate a complicated event, to spark debate, and to show the human perspective behind the world's most significant happenings of recent decades.

INTRODUCTION

Colin Powell insisted on war the right way. As a young man in the US Army in the 1960s, Powell had served in the Vietnam War. This was a conflict that did not turn out well. The United States suffered tens of thousands of casualties, while large numbers of Americans back home said they could see no purpose in the fighting. After years of severe but inconclusive warfare, US forces pulled out and their South Vietnamese allies were defeated.

Powell, wounded twice in that conflict, stayed in the Army and rose through the ranks. Under President George H.W. Bush, Powell was the United States' top man in uniform—chairman of the Joint Chiefs of Staff. By then he had formed what became known as the Powell Doctrine.

The doctrine, in essence, said military action should be used only as a last resort and only if the intended target poses a clear risk to national security; the military force brought to bear should be overwhelmingly stronger than the enemy's; the American public must strongly support the military campaign; and there must be a clear exit strategy. In short, fight only when necessary, and then make sure you win.

In 1990, that was how Powell went about his job after Iraqi president Saddam Hussein took over Kuwait by force and threatened much of the rest of the Middle East. Powell masterminded the massive buildup of US military power in the Persian Gulf and their coordination with allies' forces in what was known as Operation Desert Shield. Then, in early 1991, when Saddam would not back down, Powell oversaw Operation Desert Storm, the brutally efficient allied military campaign that won the Persian Gulf War in less than two months.

The war showcased the Powell Doctrine on a global scale and the US military reigned supreme, from its high-tech aerial weaponry to the lethal capability of its well-trained ground troops. A decade later, though, Powell was again in high position in Washington, D.C., Saddam Hussein was still provoking international discord as Iraqi president, and the United States was on its way into another war in the Persian Gulf, a war that turned out to be nowhere near as clear-cut as the first one.

Powell was now secretary of state under Bush's son, President George W. Bush. Even with his long military background and his successful leadership of the Persian Gulf War, Powell now stressed the value of diplomacy in settling the current confrontational problems. But on the question of what to do about Iraq, Powell was overruled by other top members of the Bush administration, and the new war began in 2003. Powell resigned as secretary of state a few days after the younger Bush's reelection in 2004. The later war did not fit the Powell Doctrine.

Powell said later, "I tried to avoid this war." He said that, without success, he had outlined for Bush "the consequences of going into an Arab country and becoming the occupiers."

A big question in hindsight was whether the allied forces should have ousted Saddam Hussein back in 1991. With the Iraqi military badly beaten then, shouldn't the United States have gone on into the capital, Baghdad, and taken complete control of the country?

Writing in the *Washington Post*, Rick Atkinson said, "No American military decision since the Vietnam War provoked more controversy, more debate, more caustic commentary, than the choice to offer Iraq a merciful clemency." In autumn of 1991, two-thirds of Americans surveyed said the war had ended too soon. Yet ousting, if not killing, Saddam and his top echelon would have left

Iraq leaderless and thus needing a US-run government for some period of time. That would have been the kind of occupation Powell later warned against—and that happened in the mid-2000s after the second war against Saddam.

Some have said the US forces stopped when they did so that Iraqi insurgents could knock Saddam out themselves. In fact, though, the United States did not do what it could have done to enable such a rebellion. Instead, it appears the quiet hope on the US side was that a moderate Iraqi general or group of officers would remove Saddam in an orderly coup. This would have provided Iraq with a stable and homegrown government that, most likely, the United States could have dealt with successfully.

It didn't happen.

The public arguments in favor of the quicker end to the war were mainly that a prolonged assault on the rest of Iraq would have killed many more civilians, created devastation for the survivors, and lost international support. The thinking was that, after the winning side displayed its mercy, the United Nations (UN) could help engineer a transition in Iraq that would move Saddam out of power and enable the country to become more peaceful.

The UN methods included economic sanctions against Saddam's regime and inspection teams attempting to monitor and diminish Iraq's weaponry. The effort to use diplomacy had succeeded in recruiting not only the usual US allies but such militant Arab governments as Syria.

In addition, it was noted that the reason so many nations had joined the military force that defeated Iraq was to get Iraq out of Kuwait, not to change Iraq's government. The latter result would have pleased many, of course, but the agreed-on goal was Kuwait's liberation. Once that happened, the cease-fire began.

At the time, the United States needed European and other allies to help deal with the breakup of the Soviet Union and fragmenting of Eastern Europe. It was not a good time to alienate the forces of moderation. In fact, substantial gains toward diminishing several longstanding conflicts were achieved through international cooperation in the years right after the Persian Gulf War ended.

Besides, it now looked easy enough to pound on Saddam again if necessary. There was a prevailing opinion that the US military could do whatever it wanted, wherever and whenever. Look how it had demolished the world's fourth-largest army on Iraq's home territory in just forty-odd days—and just a few days of full-scale ground warfare. Look at the dramatic power and high technology the United States deployed in the air. Victory seemed almost as easy as winning a video game.

But the war was in fact hard, even for the well-equipped US ground troops. Molly Moore, who was with the Marines who fought their way into Iraqi-held Kuwait, wrote in *A Woman at War*:

> The world came to view the war as a quick and effort-less victory by the American armed forces. To the men and women who fought it and the commanders who directed it, there was nothing easy about the ground war. . . . The brevity of the war and the relatively low number of American casualties does not diminish the intensity of the battles fought, the tragedy of those who died, or the heroism of those who risked their lives to save others.

Nor was the situation as simple in other aspects as many people thought. Had Arab nations allowed a major war they could have prevented? Was such use of force justifiable? Were the battles fought in accordance with the ethical standards of warfare, or were war crimes committed? Did individual participants do their best under stress? Did the outcome provide a structure for Mideast peace? Were a vast number of American troops poisoned? And did the public know the true story as the war happened?

The viewpoints that follow in *Perspectives on Modern World History: The Persian Gulf War* provide valuable insights and facts about one of world history's major turning points.

World Map

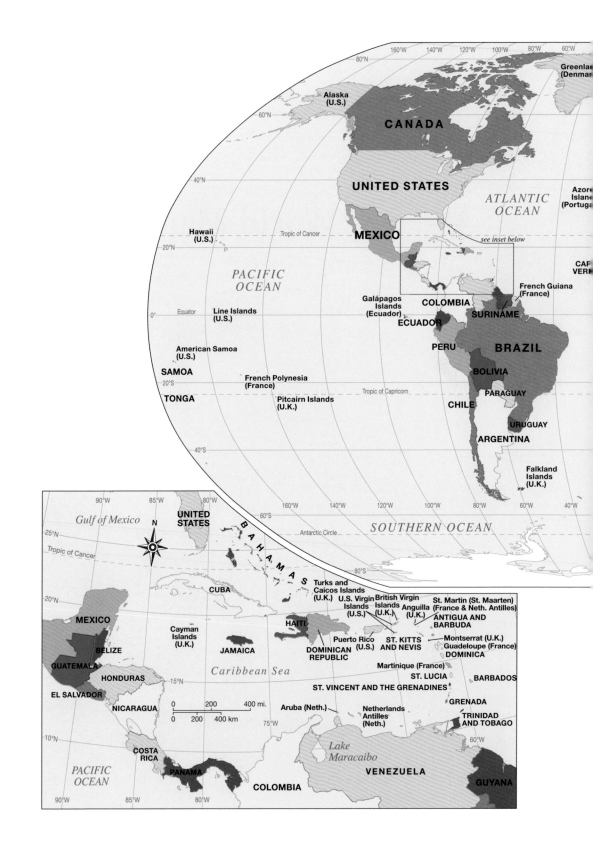

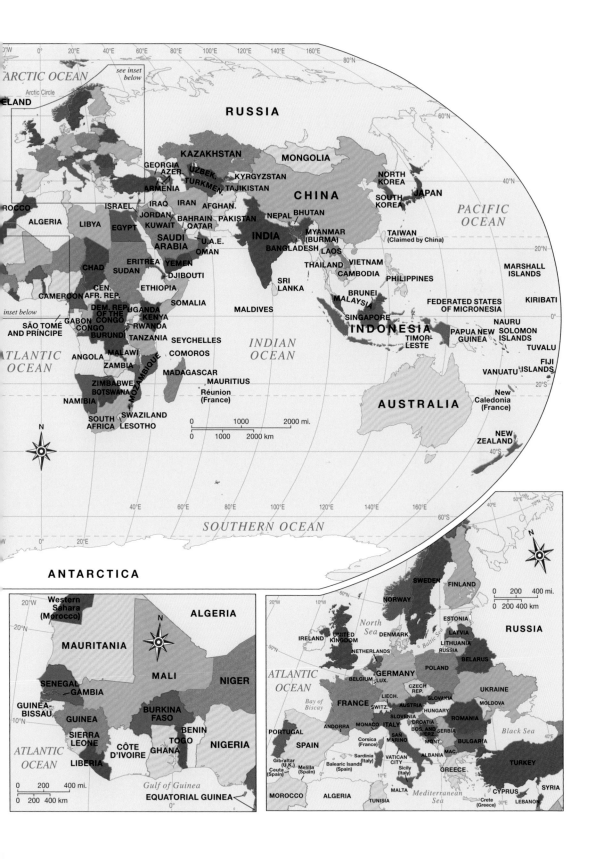

CHAPTER 1

Historical Background on the Persian Gulf War

An Overview of the War and Its Causes

Anthony H. Cordesman

With his country deep in debt after war with Iran during the 1980s, Iraq's president Saddam Hussein decided to capture the wealth of Kuwait, according to this summary by a Mideast expert. Saddam calculated his Arab neighbors and the West would not risk war in response. But in a remarkable show of unity, asserts the author, much of the world supported the assembly of a massive, mobile, and superior force led by the United States. The following viewpoint details how the international coalition crushed the Iraqi forces. Anthony H. Cordesman, of the Center for Strategic and International Studies, has been a national security analyst for ABC News and has served in the US departments of Defense, State, and Energy. He is the author of numerous studies on the Middle East.

Photo on previous page: Explosions lit up the night sky during an air attack on Baghdad by US warplanes on January 18, 1991. (**Associated Press.**)

SOURCE. Anthony H. Cordesman, "Gulf War, 1991," *International Military and Defense Encyclopedia.* © 1993 Gale, a part of Cengage Learning, Inc. Reproduced by permission of Cengage Learning. www.cengage.com/permissions.

Iraq's invasion of Kuwait on 1 August 1990 triggered a series of events that led to one of the largest-scale conflicts of the modern era. Although the actual fighting lasted only 43 days, it involved massive air and armored operations and the widespread use of new military technologies ranging from stealth attack aircraft to modern tank fire-control systems with thermal imaging sights.

> *Unlike most conflicts, Iraq's invasion of Kuwait was an act of naked aggression with little political justification or sophistication.*

The war also marked a major shift in East-West relations and within the developing world itself. It became a contest between a regional super-power, under the leadership of an ambitious dictator, and a broad coalition of United Nations [UN] forces, led by the United States and Saudi Arabia and operating in a political context where the United States had the political support of the Soviet Union. As such, it may well have been the first conflict of the post-cold war era.

Unlike most conflicts, Iraq's invasion of Kuwait was an act of naked aggression with little political justification or sophistication. In the period before the invasion, Iraq claimed that Kuwait was violating its oil quotas and improperly draining oil from the Rumalia oil field—a large reservoir largely in Iraq but whose southern tip is in Kuwait. In fact, Iraq had never agreed to a quota of its own, and most of Kuwait's modest production from the Rumalia field had gone to sales that aided Iraq during its war with Iran (1980–88). Further, Kuwait had provided Iraq with billions of dollars in aid during that war, and had offered both to cut its exports and halt production from the Rumalia field before the Iraqi invasion.

Iraq also undermined any justifications for its actions during the first days of the invasion when it first claimed to be supporting a nonexistent uprising by prodemocratic Kuwaiti forces, stated that it was withdrawing from the country but then moved toward outright annexation, and sent its forces to Kuwait's southern border with Saudi Arabia.

While Iraq then claimed it was simply liberating territory stolen from it by Britain, these claims had equally little historical justification: Iraq had no claim to Kuwait as a successor state because modern Iraq had been created by Britain after the collapse of the Turkish Empire at the end of World War I. Even the Turkish Empire had had an uncertain claim to Kuwait, since it exercised only limited or dual jurisdiction over the area, and Kuwait had normally existed as a small independent Bedouin settlement on the Persian Gulf coast. Kuwait's boundaries as a city-state were set by the British in the 1920s, and only in reaction to the threat of a Saudi invasion.

The true causes of Iraq's invasion were a mixture of economic problems and the ambitions of Saddam Hussein. Under Saddam's leadership, Iraq had continued to expand its military machine after the cease-fire in August 1988. It did so even though it had obtained more than US $60 billion worth of arms during 1980–88, and the war had cost Iraq as much as one-third of its gross domestic product. Further, Iraq was spending additional billions on missiles and biological, chemical, and nuclear weapons. At the same time, Iraq spent billions on ambitious civil development projects like the reconstruction of Basra and Al Fao.

This saddled Iraq with a foreign debt of some US $80–$100 billion at a time when oil prices were depressed and there was a significant world surplus of oil exports. As a result, Iraq could not continue to pay for its military machine, could not meet its debt payments, and experienced steadily greater problems in giving its people the kind of economic development and reconstruction they expected at the end of the war with Iran.

The invasion of Kuwait thus offered Saddam Hussein a means of distracting Iraq's population, a potential source of vast wealth, and the strategic asset of a deep-water port on the Persian Gulf. Kuwait's Fund for the Future had investments worth more than US $100 billion. Kuwait was capable of adding at least 2 million barrels a day of oil to Iraq's exports of roughly 3.5 million, and it offered the opportunity to increase Iraq's total oil reserves from 100 billion to 198 billion barrels (a total of nearly 25% of the world's total reserves). At the same time, it placed Iraqi forces on Saudi Arabia's border and within easy striking range. Even if Iraq did not attack Saudi Arabia's nearby oil fields and oil facilities, this strategic position gave it political and military leverage over nations that possessed an additional 28 percent of the world's total reserves.

Much of the World Unites Against Iraq

The success of Iraq's invasion depended, however, on the reaction of its neighbors, the United States, and other regional and world powers. Saddam Hussein seems to have calculated that neighboring states like Saudi Arabia would be too frightened to act and that the United States would either not send forces or not be willing to go to war. As it turned out, he fatally miscalculated the reaction of his neighbors, the United States, and the other nations of the world.

Instead of paralysis, Saudi Arabia immediately gave the Kuwaiti government-in-exile its full support and consulted with the United States. Rather than be intimidated when Iraq moved its divisions to the Saudi border, in position to invade Saudi Arabia, Saudi Arabia sought outside military aid. Further, Saudi Arabia immediately obtained the support of other Gulf Cooperation Council states—Bahrain, Oman, Qatar, and the United Arab Emirates.

President George [H.W.] Bush of the United States also acted immediately to check Iraqi aggression. Consulting with France, Britain, and many of the same allies

that had supported joint naval action in the Persian Gulf in 1987 and 1988, President Bush sent a delegation to Saudi Arabia that pledged the commitment of massive military forces to defend Saudi Arabia. At the same time, President Bush took immediate action to freeze Iraqi assets and to obtain UN support for a naval blockade of Iraq and an embargo on all Iraqi imports and exports other than medicine and food for humanitarian purposes. If Saddam Hussein counted on what he perceived to be weakness demonstrated by the U.S. withdrawal from Vietnam and Lebanon, he was proved totally mistaken. On 7 August, less than a week after the first Iraqi troops entered Kuwait, the United States announced it would send land, air, and naval forces to Saudi Arabia.

Most of the rest of the world proved equally decisive. Britain, France, the other members of the North Atlantic

Iraqi leaders claimed that Kuwait improperly drew oil from the Rumalia oil fields in southern Iraq, leading to Iraq's justification for war. Many years after the Gulf War, British soldiers still patrol the area. (**Associated Press.**)

Treaty Organization (NATO), Japan, most Eastern European nations, and the Soviet Union immediately joined in condemning Iraq's actions. While the Soviet Union jockeyed for political position and made its own efforts to seek Iraqi withdrawal from Kuwait, it consistently supported the United States in the United Nations and never gave Iraq any support for its actions. Most of the remaining Arab world proved equally firm. On 3 August 1990, the Arab League Council voted to condemn Iraq and demand its withdrawal from Kuwait. Egypt and Syria strongly opposed Iraq and sent military forces to defend Saudi Arabia and liberate Kuwait. So did other Arab states including Algeria. Only Jordan, Libya, Mauritania, the PLO [Palestine Liberation Organization], the Sudan, and Yemen gave Iraq significant political support during any point of the crisis.

The shift toward cooperation between East and West had an equally important impact in allowing the United Nations to take unprecedented action against Iraq. On 2 August 1990, the Security Council voted 14 to 0 (Resolution 660) to demand Iraq's immediate and unconditional withdrawal from Kuwait. The Security Council then passed resolutions that ordered a financial and trade embargo against Iraq (6 August), declared Iraq's annexation of Kuwait null and void (9 August), demanded that Iraq free all the foreign hostages it had taken (18 August), established an international naval blockade (25 August), halted all air cargo shipments (25 September), declared Iraq liable for all war damages and economic costs (29 October), and authorized the nations allied with Kuwait "to use all necessary means" if Iraq did not withdraw from Kuwait by 15 January 1991 (29 November).

For the first time since the Korean War [1950–53], the United Nations was allowed freedom of action in checking an aggressor. As a result, Iraq suffered a complete naval and economic blockade, could not export oil, and lost any access to arms imports. Its economic and military strength was severely under-mined, and it was forced to deploy a steadily increasing portion of its best forces to defend the Saudi-Kuwaiti border and its border with Saudi Arabia. By the UN deadline, Iraq had sent 545,000 men and 12 armored (heavy) and 31 mechanized infantry (light) divisions to the Kuwaiti the-ater of operations. . . .

> For the first time since the Korean War, the United Nations was allowed freedom of action in checking an aggressor.

US Dominance in the Air Was Quick and Total

The 1991 Gulf War began on 17 January 1991 when U.S.-led air units launched a devastating series of attacks on targets in Iraq. These targets included command and control facilities, communications systems, air bases, and land-based air defenses. The war began when AH-64 Apache attack helicopters knocked out Iraq's forward radar system. The United States then used F-117 stealth attack fighters, which flew 31 percent of the attacks dur-ing the first day and attacked even heavily defended targets such as downtown Baghdad with complete impu-nity. They also involved the first significant use of sea-launched cruise missiles and a wide range of precision-guided weapons.

As early as the third day of the war, the coalition air forces were able to shift their attacks from Iraq's main air defenses to such strategic targets as key headquarters, civil and army communications, electric power plants, and Iraq's plants and facilities for the production of bio-logical, chemical, and nuclear warfare.

The coalition also took full advantage of its mo-nopoly on long-range reconnaissance, photo and signal intelligence from satellites, electronic intelligence aircraft, refueling capability, air control and warning aircraft (AWACS), and sophisticated targeting aircraft like the

JSTARS. This gave it further advantages in both air-to-air and air-to-ground combat.

The advantage in air-to-air combat became clear during the first days of the war. Iraq had 770 combat aircraft, 24 main operating bases, 30 dispersal bases, and a massive network of some 3,000 surface-to-air missiles when the coalition attacked. Coalition air forces, however, were so superior that Iraq was unable to win a single air-to-air engagement and lost a total of 35 aircraft in air-to-air combat. By the end of the first week of the air war, Iraq ceased to attempt active resistance in the air, and Iraqi aircraft began to flee to Iran in hopes that Iran would return the aircraft and pilots after the war. Iraq halted even token efforts to use its aircraft in combat after the fourteenth day of the air war, and Iraq's land-based air defenses then proved vulnerable to electronic warfare, infrared and other countermeasures, and antiradiation missiles throughout the rest of the war. . . .

Almost from the outset of the war, Iraq realized it had no way to retaliate against the coalition's attacks except to launch its long-range modified Scud missile. Iraq began these missile strikes by attacking Israel and Saudi Arabia on the second day of the war and persisted in them until the cease-fire. Iraq launched a total of 40 Scud variants against Israel and 46 against Saudi Arabia, but these missiles never succeeded in doing major military damage. They also failed to provoke Israel into retaliating against Iraq, largely because the United States rushed Patriot defense missiles to both Israel and Saudi Arabia; the Patriot's ability to hit most incoming Scuds provided a vital boost in public confidence. Israeli restraint may have played a key role in ensuring that the Arab members of the coalition continued to support it throughout the war. . . .

> Iraq realized it had no way to retaliate against the coalition's attacks except to launch its long-range modified Scud missile.

By the time the ground war began at 0400 hours on 24 February 1991, Iraqi ground forces had been hit by more than 40,000 attack sorties. While the resulting damage estimates are controversial, coalition airpower claimed to have destroyed or severely damaged: all of Iraq's nuclear reactor facilities, eleven chemical and biological weapons storage facilities and three production facilities, 60 percent of Iraq's major command centers, 70 percent of its military communications, 125 ammunition storage revetments, 48 Iraqi naval vessels, and 75 percent of Iraq's electric power-generating capability. Logistic supply to the theater had been cut by up to 90 percent, and the U.S. command estimated that at least 1,300 Iraqi tanks, 800 other armored vehicles, and 1,100 artillery pieces had been destroyed from the air.

These air attacks continued throughout the air-land phase of the war that followed. By the cease-fire of 28 February, coalition air forces had dropped a total of 88,500 tons of ordnance, of which 6,520 tons were precision-guided weapons. A total of 216 Iraqi aircraft had been destroyed, along with nearly 600 aircraft shelters. Coalition air forces had also destroyed 54 bridges or made them inoperable—playing a major role in cutting off Iraqi land forces from their final route of escape along the Tigris [River] north of Basra during the last days of the war.

On the Ground, the Coalition Prevailed Readily

Once the ground phase of the war began, it proved to be extraordinarily quick and decisive. The coalition not only attacked a gravely weakened Iraqi army and had a massive advantage in intelligence and virtually every area of tactical technology, it had vastly superior tactics. The coalition forces used the "air-land battle" concept, which the United States had developed to meet the Warsaw Pact's most modern forces in Europe, against an Iraqi force that was equipped with modern weapons but had trained and organized to fight a relatively static trench war against an Iran that lacked significant airpower.

While coalition land forces did not enjoy a significant superiority in weapons strength and manpower over Iraq, they did consist largely of highly motivated professionals. In contrast, the majority of Iraqi forces were poorly trained conscripts who seemed to have poor morale and little motivation. It is impossible to determine how much of this weakness stemmed from having to invade an Arab "brother," poor leadership and organization, or the coalition's air attacks. All three combined to undermine Iraqi military capabilities.

Iraq's one "success" in the land war occurred long before coalition land forces began to liberate Kuwait. Several Iraqi brigades made a brief incursion into the Saudi border town of Khafji on 29 January. But the town had been evacuated, and the Iraqi forces were driven back the next day by Saudi, Qatari, and U.S. Marine forces. The net result was that Iraq did more to reveal its weaknesses than advance its own cause.

The attack on Khafji also did nothing to keep coalition land forces from making a massive shift from positions along the coast and to the south of Kuwait, to areas near the Iraqi-Saudi border to the west of Kuwait. These shifts later allowed coalition land forces to drive deep into Iraq and Kuwait.

The shifts of land forces began on 17 January, the same day the air phase of the war began. They involved massive logistic and movement difficulties, but they eventually positioned the U.S. Marine Expeditionary Force and Saudi, Syrian, and Egyptian forces where they could drive north from the center of Kuwait's southern border toward Kuwait City. At the same time, French and U.S. forces in VII Corps moved far to the west, where they could launch an attack to cut off southern Iraq from Baghdad and then drive around Kuwait to move against

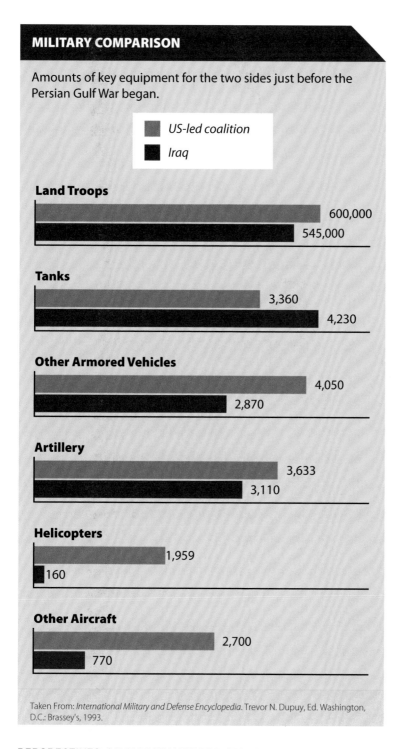

MILITARY COMPARISON

Amounts of key equipment for the two sides just before the Persian Gulf War began.

US-led coalition

Iraq

Land Troops

600,000

545,000

Tanks

3,360

4,230

Other Armored Vehicles

4,050

2,870

Artillery

3,633

3,110

Helicopters

1,959

160

Other Aircraft

2,700

770

Taken From: *International Military and Defense Encyclopedia.* Trevor N. Dupuy, Ed. Washington, D.C.: Brassey's, 1993.

Basra from the west. British and U.S. Army forces in XVIII Corps moved to areas on the Saudi-Iraqi border just west of Kuwait.

In a move he later called his "Hail Mary play," the allied commander, Gen. Norman Schwartzkopf, was able to position two full armored corps along the Iraqi border to the west of Kuwait without the Iraqis detecting these movements. He was able to keep them undetected through the use of special forces and extensive frontline patrols, and because coalition airpower denied Iraq any air reconnaissance capability, even near its own border.

This element of surprise played a key role when the air-land battle began on 24 February 1991. Two major simultaneous attacks quickly crossed Iraqi defensive positions. The first consisted of Pan-Arab (Saudi, Kuwaiti, Qatari, and Omani) forces and U.S. Marine forces attacking on a broad front from the northern "notch" in the Saudi-Kuwaiti border to the coast and penetrating the Iraqi defenses along the southern Kuwait border. These forces advanced as far as half the distance to Kuwait City within twelve hours. This attack was aided by the fact that many of Iraq's forces were kept pinned down by a U.S. deception operation that convinced Iraqi commanders that U.S. Marine amphibious forces might strike at any point along the coast.

The second attack occurred at the far western edge of coalition positions along the Iraqi-Saudi border. The French 6th Light Armored Division and one brigade of the 82d Airborne Division drove 90 miles north to seize an airfield at Al-Salman. The U.S. 101st Airborne Division then launched the largest air assault operation in military history, and U.S. heliborne forces moved first to a forward logistic base in Iraq and then to positions

> The U.S. 101st Airborne Division then launched the largest air assault operation in military history.

near Samawah on the Euphrates [River]. This attack cut Iraqi forces off from the main routes from Basra to Baghdad that run south of the Euphrates.

The coalition attacked along a third major line that same afternoon. The 3d Armored and 24th divisions of XVIII Corps drove across the Iraqi border and toward the Wadi al-Batin and the western approaches to Kuwait City. Immediately to the east, U.S. and British land forces also advanced into Iraq. The 1st U.S. Division forced a breach in the Iraqi defenses that was rapidly exploited by the 1st British Armored Division and the 2d Cavalry Regiment and 1st and 3d Armored divisions of the U.S. Army. This advance rapidly turned into a deep thrust against the Republican Guard forces west of Kuwait City, north of Kuwait, and west of Basra. Finally, Egyptian and Saudi forces, backed by Syrian fire support, launched a fourth attack on Iraqi positions to the east of the gorge of Al-Batin on the 25th.

These attacks, and the relentless air attacks that had preceded them, quickly shattered the remaining organization, morale, and war-fighting capability of most of the Iraqi army, while the Republican Guards remained pinned down outside Kuwait. As a result, coalition forces were able to drive up through Kuwait to strike positions south and west of Kuwait City, while VII and XVIII Corps forces moved deep into Iraq, to positions south of a line drawn from the border to Nasiryah.

Overwhelming Victory Came Rapidly

On 26 February, forces of VII and XVIII Corps closed on the Iraqi Republican Guard forces and reserves defending Basra in the longest sustained armored advance in history. They destroyed the key Republican Guard divisions holding the area just north of the Kuwaiti border. Other coalition forces, including the 1st and 2d Marine Divisions, reached positions on the edge of Kuwait City and began fighting for control of the international airport. These advances took place despite extraordinarily bad weather, which created substantial amounts of mud and interfered with air cover.

The war ended with a devastating series of engagements where Iraqi forces were able to put up only limited resistance. The thermal sights and superior fire-control systems of coalition tanks allowed them to achieve massive kills against Iraqi armor, backed by lethal systems like the AH-64 attack helicopter and the Multiple Launch Rocket System. The coalition's vastly superior intelligence and night vision devices, combined with the use of new navigation aids that provided precise location data from global positioning satellites, gave its land forces control of both the desert and the night. . . .

The scale of the coalition's success in fighting a 1,000-hour air battle and the 100-hour air-land battle that followed is indicated by the fact that coalition land forces succeeded in reaching every major objective ahead of schedule and with far fewer casualties than their commanders dared to hope for. They achieved a rate of advance so fast that many units did not bother to halt at their intermediate objectives.

The scale of the coalition's success is also indicated by U.S. estimates that coalition forces had destroyed nearly 4,000 Iraqi tanks, more than 1,000 other armored vehicles, and nearly 3,000 artillery weapons. In contrast, the coalition suffered combat losses of four tanks, nine other armored vehicles, and one artillery weapon. Although coalition aircraft flew a total of 109,876 sorties by the end of the war, the coalition lost only 38 aircraft—the lowest loss rate of any air combat in history and less than the normal accident rate per sortie in combat training. The difference in manpower losses is even more astounding, although no precise estimates are possible. U.S. intelligence issued rough estimates after the war that 100,000 Iraqi soldiers died in combat. Allied killed—less casualties to friendly fire—totaled less than 200.

How Saddam Hussein Prepared for the War

Lawrence Freedman and Efraim Karsh

By taking over the country of Kuwait, Iraq's president Saddam Hussein took his chances on whether a US-led coalition would try to oust him militarily, the authors of the following viewpoint write. Saddam calculated that his military strength and defenses, combined with the United States' reluctance to see its troops die in a foreign cause, would mean no war. But, the authors claim, he was not realistic about his vulnerability. Lawrence Freedman is a professor of war studies at King's College, London, and author of such books as *U.S. Intelligence and the Soviet Strategic Threat*. Efraim Karsh, a lecturer in the same King's College department, is well known as a writer on the Middle East and in particular the Iran-Iraq war.

SOURCE. Lawrence Freedman and Efraim Karsh, *The Gulf Conflict: 1990–1991.* © 1993 by Lawrence Freedman and Efraim Karsh. Published by Princeton University Press. Reproduced by permission.

For Saddam [Hussein, president of Iraq], all the proposals for a diplomatic solution [to Iraq's occupation of Kuwait] sweetened a very bitter pill with only a small amount of sugar. The only certain part was Iraq's withdrawal from Kuwait. Western pledges not to attack were firm, but these were the sort of promises he had made himself in the past to others and then ignored. If Saddam withdrew with his military power intact, then other actors in the area—including Kuwait—would want a continued Western presence and he would judge himself to be at continual risk. A partial withdrawal, by which he relinquished all of Kuwait other than, for example, one of the islands, would be of little help. It might help hold off war but was unlikely to see sanctions lifted and so provided no economic relief. If the withdrawal was not part of an agreed deal, then the fortifications from around the perimeter of Kuwait would be abandoned, exposing Iraqi forces in the process. Giving an inch in Kuwait would reveal a lack of confidence in the long-term position and the pressure to complete the withdrawal would be unremitting.

The idea of an international conference on the Arab-Israeli and other disputes, on which so many third parties pinned their hopes, never stood any real chance of enticing Iraq out of Kuwait. Not once did Saddam even imply that it was worth the release of Kuwait. . . . He did not even refer to such a conference. What he meant by linkage was that the Palestinian problem (as well as the Syrian presence in Lebanon) would have to be *resolved*, and not merely addressed, before the Kuwaiti issue could be tackled. Given the complexity of these problems and the lengthy time required for their resolution, the concrete consequence of Saddam's 'linkage' was that he would be given an indefinite respite to 'Iraqize' Kuwait, while at the same time gaining enormous prestige in the Arab world. The vague prospect of a conference after he had been obliged to relinquish Kuwait never interested

Saddam. As he could not be seen to be withdrawing simply because of American pressure, he had little choice but to prepare himself for war.

By the start of 1991, Saddam should have been aware that the coalition was more cohesive than expected: calls for popular insurrections against its Arab members had produced a minimal response; the attempt to wean France away through preferential release of hostages had failed; the Soviet Union had supported a series of tough anti-Iraq resolutions in the UN [United Nations] including Resolution 678. Nonetheless Saddam still apparently hoped that the peace camp in the West, and the variety of would-be intermediaries still visiting him in Baghdad, would help him avert war. It was an almost fatalistic approach, wholly dependent upon political calculations in Washington [D.C.] which he could influence only by making any war seem as terrible as possible.

His residual hope that war might be avoided meant that apparently no serious consideration was given to a pre-emptive attack on coalition forces in Saudi Arabia to disrupt and confuse their preparations. The classic reason against pre-emption is that it makes inevitable what was before merely probable and can be used to justify terrible retribution. In addition it would have required a bold offensive plan at a time when, in military terms, Saddam was in a defensive frame of mind. His land forces were in no position to move forward. Any offensives were going to be essentially political in nature and designed to play on the supposed American intolerance of casualties and the disinclination of Arab members of the coalition to fight another state engaged in a conflict with Israel.

An Attempt to Play on American Fears

The military requirement was to deter, and if necessary rebuff, the

'Yours is a society which cannot accept 10,000 dead in one battle.'

Ultimate Weaponry

Going nuclear was not beyond Saddam Hussein's grasp. In 1971, he ordered a scientific team to work on creating nuclear bombs, according to *Saddam's Bombmaker,* a book by his former director of the program, Khidhir Hamza. The work went on both before and after the Persian Gulf War, and came very close to succeeding, said Hamza, who fled Iraq in 1994. The aim had been to make a half-dozen bombs a year.

Just before the war began, Saddam also considered a package deal for nuclear weapons designs, production plants and foreign experts, according to another book, *Peddling Peril: How the Secret Nuclear Trade Arms America's Enemies.* Under this deal, according to author David Albright, Iraq would have paid $150 million to the brilliant rogue Pakistani scientist Abdul Qadeer Khan.

central thrust of the enemy campaign while absorbing the enemy air assault. There was no obvious strategy for war termination other than inflicting such discomfort that the coalition would develop an interest in a cease-fire on terms other than the full implementation of all UN resolutions. Saddam strongly believed that the United States's Achilles' heel [fatal weakness] was its extreme sensitivity to casualties, and he was determined to exploit this weakness to the full. As he told the American Ambassador to Baghdad, April Glaspie, shortly before the invasion of Kuwait: 'Yours is a society which cannot accept 10,000 dead in one battle,' as if the fact this might be the case with Iraq was some sort of recommendation. A constant theme in the Iraqi media was the evidence of Vietnam that public opinion would resent deaths in the desert and could not cope with the demands of a long war—which, they warned, was much more likely than the few weeks anticipated in the American press.

Saddam's awareness that a war might have to be fought could be seen on 12 December 1990, when the Iraqi Minister of Defence, General Abd al-Jabbar Khalil Shanshal, was replaced by Lieutenant General Sa'di Tumah Abbas, a seasoned veteran of the Iran-Iraq War. An elderly professional soldier of a rather taciturn personality, Shanshal had assumed his position in mid 1989, following the mysterious death in a helicopter accident of the then Minister of Defence, Adnan Khairallah Talfah, Saddam's cousin. It had been clear from the beginning that Shanshal's appointment was temporary, designed to eliminate mutterings of discontent in the military regarding the cause of Adnan's death. His removal at that particular stage in the crisis, however, was illustrative of Saddam's growing conviction of the imminence of war.

Another indication was the intensification of the regime's hectic efforts to improve Iraq's military and civilian preparedness. Saddam held several well-publicized meetings with the military and the political leadership. Peasants, who at the beginning of the crisis had been exempted from military service as a means to combat the economic sanctions, were ordered to report immediately to their units. The public was given elaborate instructions regarding self-protection against chemical and nuclear attacks, and told to black out homes and to store a medicine cabinet in every apartment. Individuals and institutions were ordered to clear their shelters for immediate use, and to store oil products for an emergency. Civil defence drills were held, including a large-scale exercise of an evacuation of Baghdad, involving hundreds of thousands of people.

The expectations of war were also reflected in the references of the Iraqi mass media to the crisis. Alongside the already standard doomsday scenarios of a 'second

Vietnam', and threats to draw Israel into the conflict, a sombre, perhaps even apologetic, tone crept into the official commentaries. The Iraqi people were asked to brace themselves for yet another imposed war which was not of their leadership's choice. 'Iraq has given peace every chance it deserved, and has repeatedly proved that it was seeking peace,' argued the Iraqi press, 'but given the US-Western insistence on war and aggression, Iraq will not hesitate to engage in confrontation and fighting to destroy the invading forces.' And Saddam put his acceptance of the inevitability of war in a somewhat fatalistic fashion: 'If it is God Almighty's will that we fight this battle to cleanse the Arab homeland of all this rottenness, so be it.'

> Saddam seemingly hoped that the loss of Kuwait in a war with the allies would make him a hero, lauded by the Arab masses.

The die had been cast. Saddam's mind seemed to have been made up. War would not have been his first choice. However, caught between the risks of unconditional withdrawal and the risks but also the opportunities of an armed confrontation, the choice seemed self-evident. Were he to succeed in holding on against the coalition for some time, war would offer Saddam the best chance for political survival and even a final victory. The concessions available in pre-war negotiation were inferior to those that might be obtained as a result of battle. In addition, just as the Egyptian President Gamal Abd al-Nasser had managed to turn his country's military defeat in the 1956 Suez campaign, against a Franco-Anglo-Israeli coalition, into a resounding political victory, so Saddam seemingly hoped that the loss of Kuwait in a war with the allies would make him a hero, lauded by the Arab masses as a new Nasser, a leader who defied world imperialism and survived.

Given this apparent state of mind, a last-minute reversal in the Iraqi position was inconceivable. Saddam's readiness to send [Iraqi leader] Tariq Aziz to Geneva and to meet [Peruvian diplomat] Perez de Cuellar in Baghdad was in each case a propaganda ploy, not unlike his agreement to hold the Jeddah [Saudi Arabia] talks with the Kuwaitis prior to the invasion of the emirate. He appeared to have suspected that [US president] George [H.W.] Bush had proposed the Geneva meeting only due to Congressional pressures, and that he would offer Iraq nothing except an unconditional withdrawal. It was also an open secret that the UN Secretary-General was constrained by Security Council resolutions. These avenues had to be followed to convince Iraqis that the war they were about to face, merely two years after the end of the prolonged confrontation with Iran, was the result of American intransigence. On 14 January the Iraqi National Assembly endorsed Saddam Hussein's determination to fight. It called on the Iraqi people to 'proceed towards holy jihad', and gave its absolute leader 'full constitutional authority to deal with all that is necessitated by the decisive confrontation to preserve the right and dignity of Iraq and the Arab nation'. Iraq was ready for war.

Behind the Barricades Was a Vulnerable Force

A strategy of intensive defence, conceding no ground without a hard fight, was Saddam's best hope of achieving his political objective of holding on to as much of Kuwait as possible. The higher the costs imposed, the more the enemy would be prepared to accept a peace on terms that were unobtainable prior to hostilities.

To this end, Iraqi forces barricaded themselves into Kuwait. They constructed a massive defensive line close to the border with Saudi Arabia, a mixture of obstacles designed to stop a tank offensive, with coastal defences prepared for an amphibious assault. The barricade was supplemented by playing on a variety of other fears prevalent in the coalition—of the general destructiveness and uncontrollability of war, of a readiness to resort to chemical warfare or to extend the war to Israel, of an accompanying barrage of terrorist incidents, of ecological horrors consequent on the mining of the wellheads in the Kuwait oilfields. Saddam must bet on his enemy, when faced with all this, breaking before he did. So long as he still controlled part of Kuwait he would be happy to agree to calls for a cease-fire at any time.

Saddam appeared to draw comfort from the war with Iran. However, the persistence of this struggle had not been Saddam's choice, but imposed by a fanatical foe openly demanding his downfall. He survived the war largely by shielding the Iraqi public from its effects. Iran's inability to extend the war to the Iraqi rear, combined with generous financial help from the Gulf states, allowed Saddam to keep it confined to the battlefield and to preserve, by and large, an atmosphere of 'business as usual' for the Iraqi population. Whenever Iran had managed to reach the Iraqi home front during the so-called Wars of the Cities, Saddam had quickly backed down. The Iraqi Air Force had been ineffective in close air support and the pilots were judged to be poor. The chain of command was heavily centralized and unresponsive. With regard to battle experience, Generals who had made their names in the war with Iran were retired, dead or under arrest.

> Generals who had made their names in the [Iran-Iraq War] were retired, dead or under arrest.

Even Iraq's much celebrated defensive prowess was overstated. Iraqi military operations during the Iran-Iraq War had been conducted under ideal circumstances, with superior firepower and complete mastery of the air. Still defences had been repeatedly breached by the ill-equipped Iranian teenagers, whose advance had been contained with great difficulty and, at times, through the use of chemical weapons. If Iran had not been severed from its main arms suppliers and if Saddam had not enjoyed support from large sections of the international community, he would have lost. The mobilized reservists—now half the total Iraqi force—had shown a readiness to surrender when the opportunity arose.

Saddam could call upon a large number of reserves. Iraq's overall population was not large at 19 million, but he could put together an army of some 1 million men, because the country had been on a war footing for nearly a decade. It was not quite 'the fourth largest army in the world', as the Pentagon described it, but it was nonetheless substantial. The settlement reached with Iran after the invasion of Kuwait allowed the shift of a number of divisions from that border. As the crisis developed, and in particular after Bush's announcement of the US build-up on 8 November, the number of divisions was boosted. On 19 November Saddam announced that he was reinforcing with another 250,000 men (although he was unable actually to achieve this). All young men were called up, to be followed by the middle-aged, and then given extra pay to keep them from grumbling.

Hussein's Geographical Considerations

There does seem to have been some belief that large numbers of defenders would have a deterrent effect. In mid-November the Iraqi Armed Forces General Command claimed that

> even without considering the state of morale, the difference in supply sources, and other considerations, all of which are in Iraq's favour—if the battle starts, the wicked US administration would need a ratio of three to one to become technically able to launch an attack against the valiant and faithful God's forces. This would raise the US force requirement to 3 million.

Such reasoning reflected a mechanical belief in the famous three to one ratio, widely held by military strategists to be necessary for an attacking force against an entrenched defence. However, there was plenty of evidence from contemporary conflicts, not least the Arab-Israeli wars, that numerically inferior forces can be victorious if able to exploit qualitative or tactical advantages, such as surprise. If the ratio did have any meaning, it would only be at a local level where part of an attacking force faced well dug-in defenders.

But Saddam could not ensure a heavy concentration of defending forces *all* along the line, for he could have no confidence that the coalition would confine its attentions solely to Kuwait. In addition, significant forces had to remain deployed along Iraq's borders with its Iranian, Turkish, and Syrian neighbours. He was noticeably careful with the Republican Guard, Iraq's best equipped units, which had been expanded from a brigade in 1982 to eight divisions in 1990. With higher pay, better training and access to the best equipment, the Guard was considered to be the most professional of the Iraqi forces and the most loyal to the regime. The Guard divisions straddled the border with Kuwait operating as, at best, a strategic armoured reserve. Some units were regrouped around Baghdad to protect the Ba'th regime should either an external or an internal threat emerge in the course of the war. Saddam was anxious not to hazard the praetorian protectors of his personal rule.

Iraq Was Especially Weak in the Air

Consequently, there were not enough troops to put along a wide front and so the border defences were manned by less capable troops. The large numbers claimed by Iraq did not arrive in the Kuwait theatre. Despite Western estimates (reinforced by Iraqi statements) of at least 540,000, many divisions were well below strength. Yet even if the high numbers had been reached, the Iraqi forces would probably have been weaker rather than stronger, for the numbers deployed were something of a liability, creating a logistical nightmare. Food, fuel, equipment and ammunition would have been spread even more thinly, with the stretched supply lines from Iraq vulnerable to air strikes.

The most obvious weakness in the Iraqi military structure was the lack of air support. On the face of it, Iraq possessed the world's sixth largest air force. It was credited with some 700 combat aircraft, including the highly advanced types of MiG-29, Su-24 and Mirage-F1. Its air defence system appeared to be particularly formidable. The key role it played during the war with Iran, in breaking enemy morale through sustained campaigns against strategic targets and population centres, underscored the significance of airpower in modern war. The hardened bunkers prepared for the most valuable aircraft, the enormous airfields, and the redundant command and control system all indicated a sensitivity to the dangers of pre-emptive air attack, and presumably the central importance of airpower in Israeli strategy. Israel had, after all, attacked and destroyed Iraq's Osiraq nuclear reactor in 1981. And yet, even during the Iran-Iraq War, Saddam displayed considerable restraint in the employment of airpower, refraining for a long time from carrying Iraq's overwhelming aerial superiority to its logical end. This timidity reflected Saddam's reluctance to put at risk his most effective reserve of military force. This insecure operational concept was extended into the Kuwaiti crisis. He apparently took comfort from the failure of the Americans to win in Vietnam, even with superior airpower.

> Saddam saw missiles as his most reliable means of inflicting a painful blow at the enemy.

Another key underestimation was in the area of precision-guided weapons, with which Iraqi defences proved unable to cope. This may not have been wholly unreasonable, given that many of the most modern weapons were unproven and that their effectiveness was widely questioned even in the West, where there were many reports, following the initial Desert Shield deployments, that high-technology systems were suffering in the heat and the dust of the desert environment. In addition, the full significance of electronic warfare was imperfectly understood. Saddam saw missiles as his most reliable means of inflicting a painful blow at the enemy. Iraqi ballistic missile stocks were extensive and, with the benefit of European technology, their range had been extended and some of them were configured with chemical warheads. They represented Saddam's best prospects of taking the war into the enemy camp and so were the instruments of his political offensive, with Israel their primary targets. Missiles could also be used against Saudi population centres and, to a lesser extent, as a threat to the Saudi oil installations. Saddam's first response to Bush's 8 November announcement had been to threaten to turn Saudi Arabia into a battle zone. The fear of missile attacks on Saudi installations, which was given considerable credibility by some analysts, was in part responsible for the expectation that oil prices would rise when the war began.

Hussein's Psychological Weaponry

In a speech a few days before the war began, Saddam told an Islamic gathering in Baghdad that 'thousands of men' at the front were 'underground in strong reinforced positions', ready to 'rise against' the enemy as soon as it attacked. He acknowledged that the coming war would be a testing ground for advanced technology but stressed Iraqi numerical superiority and experience of war. The Americans would 'carry out acrobatics just like a Rambo movie . . . they tell you that the Americans have advanced missiles and warplanes, but they ought to rely on their soldiers armed with rifles and grenades'. And it is here that Iraq's numerical superiority and greater dedication would be brought to bear. Saddam sent his own message to President Bush on 16 January. If Bush believed that Iraqi ground forces could be 'neutralized', he warned, 'then you are deluding yourself and this delusion will place you in great trouble'. The coming battle would not just be a 'second Vietnam'. It would be the 'mother of all battles'.

The US President Takes Action to Oppose Iraq

George H.W. Bush

Less than three weeks after Iraq took over Kuwait by force, the US president issued the following document stating why the situation involved crucial American interests. Relevant factors included access to oil and the stability of nations in the area friendly to the United States. George H.W. Bush said he had the global legal authority to form a coalition to oust the Iraqi forces. This complete official statement outlines a range of actions to be taken—and the justifications for each. George H.W. Bush was elected the forty-first president of the United States in 1988. His single term in office included serving as the commander in chief during the Persian Gulf War.

U.S. interests in the Persian Gulf are vital to the national security. These interests include access to oil and the security and stability of key friendly states in the region. The United States will defend its

---

SOURCE. George H.W. Bush, "National Security Directive 45: US Policy in Response to the Iraqi Invasion of Kuwait," August 20, 1990.

vital interests in the area, through the use of U.S. military force if necessary and appropriate, against any power with interests inimical to our own. The United States also will support the individual and collective self-defense of friendly countries in the area to enable them to play a more active role in their own defense. The United States will encourage the effective expressions of support and the participation of our allies and other friendly states to promote our mutual interests in the Persian Gulf region.

On Thursday, August 2, 1990, the government of Iraq, without provocation or warning, invaded and occupied the State of Kuwait, thereby placing these vital U.S. interests at risk. Four principles will guide U.S. policy during this crisis:

- the immediate, complete, and unconditional withdrawal of all Iraqi forces from Kuwait;

- the restoration of Kuwait's legitimate government to replace the puppet regime installed by Iraq;

- a commitment to the security and stability of the Persian Gulf; and,

- the protection of the lives of American citizens abroad.

Bush Outlines Impending U.S. Actions

To meet these principles and to bring the crisis to an immediate, peaceful, and just end, I hereby direct that the following diplomatic, economic, energy, and military measures be undertaken.

Diplomatic. The United States will continue to support the precepts of UNSC [United Nations Security Council] Resolutions 660 and 662 condemning Iraq's invasion and subsequent annexation of Kuwait and calling for the immediate and unconditional withdrawal of Iraqi forces from Kuwait. The Secretary of State should continue to work bilaterally with our allies and friends, and in

President George H.W. Bush ordered diplomatic, military, and other measures to protect US economic interests and citizens in the Persian Gulf region. (Time & Life Pictures/Getty Images.)

concert with the international community through the United Nations [UN] and other fora, to find a peaceful solution to end the Iraqi occupation of Kuwait and to restore Kuwait's legitimate government.

Economic. Consistent with my authority under the International Emergency Economic Powers Act, the National Emergencies Act, the United Nations Participation Act, and section 301 of title 3 of the United States Code, the Executive Orders signed on August 2 and August 9, 1990, freezing Kuwaiti and Iraqi assets in this country and prohibiting transactions with Iraq and Kuwait remain

44

in force. The Secretary of the Treasury, in consultation with the Secretary of State, should continue to take such actions, including the promulgation of rules and regulations, as may be necessary to carry out the purposes of these Orders. Furthermore, the United States will continue to support UNSC Resolution 661 imposing mandatory economic sanctions against Iraq and Kuwait under Chapter VII of the United Nations Charter. We will emphasize individual and collective compliance with these sanctions, but are prepared, if necessary, to enforce them in the exercise of our inherent right of individual and collective self-defense under Article 51 of the UN Charter.

> The United States now imports nearly half the oil it consumes and, as a result of the current crisis, could face a major threat to its economy.

Energy. The United States now imports nearly half the oil it consumes and, as a result of the current crisis, could face a major threat to its economy. Much of the world is even more dependent on imported oil and more vulnerable to Iraqi threats. To minimize any impact that oil flow reductions from Iraq and Kuwait will have on the world's economies, it will be our policy to ask oil-producing nations to do what they can to increase production to offset these losses. I also direct the Secretaries of State and Energy to explore with the member countries of the International Energy Agency (IEA) a coordinated drawdown of strategic petroleum reserves, and implementation of complementary measures. I will continue to ask the American public to exercise restraint in their own consumption of oil products. The Secretary of Energy should work with various sectors of the U.S. economy to encourage energy conservation and fuel switching to non-oil sources, where appropriate and economic. Finally, I will continue to appeal to oil companies to show restraint in their pricing of crude oil and products. The Secretary of Energy, as appropriate, should work with oil companies in this regard.

Military. To protect U.S. interests in the Gulf and in response to requests from the King of Saudi Arabia and the Amir of Kuwait, I have ordered U.S. military forces deployed to the region for two purposes: to deter and, if necessary, defend Saudi Arabia and other friendly states in the Gulf region from further Iraqi aggression; and to enforce the mandatory Chapter 7 sanctions under Article 51 of the UN Charter and UNSC Resolutions 660 and 661. U.S. forces will work together with those of Saudi Arabia and other Gulf countries to preserve their national integrity and to deter further Iraqi aggression. Through their presence, as well as through training and exercises, these multinational forces will enhance the overall capability of Saudi Arabia and other regional states to defend themselves.

I also approve U.S. participation, in conjunction with the forces of other friendly governments, in two separate multinational forces that would provide for the defense of Saudi Arabia and enforce the UN mandated sanctions. These two groups will be called the Multinational Force for Saudi Arabia (MNFSA) and the Multinational Force to enforce sanctions (MNFES) against Iraq and Kuwait. The United States should coordinate closely with the Saudis, the Kuwaitis, and others on the composition and organization of these forces.

> Adequate legal basis exists . . . for the implementation of multinational efforts.

Multinational Force Operations

The MNFSA. The MNFSA is to deter aggression by Iraq against Saudi Arabia and other friendly Arab states in the Gulf, to ensure the territorial integrity and political independence of Saudi Arabia and other members of the GCC [Gulf Cooperation Council], and to conduct exercises and training to enhance the proficiency of Saudi forces in the defense of the Kingdom.

Adequate legal basis exists under the UN Charter and UNSC resolutions for the implementation of multinational efforts. I do not believe it is necessary now for the United States to seek additional UN endorsement for the MNFSA. If I subsequently determine that further UN endorsement is required, we should ensure that any UN-led effort is acceptable to U.S. military commanders and an adequate command structure is established and operating beforehand.

In concert with the other UNSC Permanent members, I authorize U.S. participation in discussions of the UN Military Staff Committee on the MNF operation for Saudi Arabia. If such talks are initiated, they should be of lower priority than talks concerning the MNFES.

Soviet participation in the MNFSA is warranted only if the Saudis request it. If so, we should work with the Saudis to insure that the Soviet mission is acceptable to us and that Soviet forces are deployed at a distance from U.S. operations in these countries. Soviet assistance in providing lift support to others providing forces inside Saudi Arabia should be encouraged.

The MNFES. The MNF to enforce economic sanctions against Iraq and Kuwait is designed to bring about the withdrawal of Iraqi forces from Kuwait, and to restore Kuwait's sovereignty, independence, and territorial integrity. Participating countries would seek to prevent the export of all commodities and products originating in Iraq or Kuwait, regardless of port of embarkation or transshipment point, and prevent the shipment to Iraq or Kuwait, regardless of declared port of destination or transshipment point, of any commodities or supplies whose provision to Iraq or Kuwait is contrary to UNSC

Resolutions 660 and 661. These efforts should complement individual and collective compliance measures already in force.

In accordance with Article 51 of the UN Charter and UNSC Resolutions 660 and 661, I hereby direct that all imports and exports, except medicines and food for humanitarian purposes (i.e., natural disasters) bound to and from Iraq and Kuwait be intercepted immediately. I direct the Secretary of Defense to immediately organize and coordinate a multinational force as requested by the Government of Kuwait. U.S. forces, in coordination with other cooperating national forces, should take necessary action to intercept vessels on a case-by-case basis until sufficient U.S. and other forces are available for more comprehensive enforcement. I also approve the submission to Congress of a separate letter informing it of the character and basis for our intercept operations in keeping with my commitment to congressional consultations on matters of national importance. The GCC states and potential contributors to the MNFES should be notified of the implementation of the intercept operation. I also agree to Soviet participation in the MNFES.

Since the UN Charter provides the legal basis for the conduct of this operation, I do not believe it is necessary now to obtain additional UN endorsement for the MNFES. Subject to the consent of the UNSC Permanent members, I agree to allow U.S. participation in discussions of the MNFES operation for enforcing sanctions against Iraq and Kuwait by the UN Military Staff Committee.

Baghdad Celebrates a New Year While on the Brink of War

Elaine Sciolino

In the months between Iraq's invasion of Kuwait and the Operation Desert Storm counterattack, the Iraqi capital, Baghdad, was a strange place, journalist Elaine Sciolino reports. Brightly lit parties contrasted with bombastic propaganda. Hope for a peaceful compromise alternated with expectations of catastrophe, she claims. Luxury items filled store shelves while prices soared for basics such as rice, sugar, milk, and flour. Supposedly captive Kuwaitis circulated freely around Baghdad. Sciolino has been a foreign correspondent based in Rome, Paris, the United Nations, and Washington, D.C. She joined the *New York Times* in 1984.

SOURCE. Elaine Sciolino, "The Mother of All Battles," *The Outlaw State: Saddam Hussein's Quest for Power and the Gulf Crisis.* Copyright © 1991 by Elaine Sciolino. Published by John Wiley & Sons, Inc. Reproduced by permission of Charlotte Sheedy Literary Agency, Inc.

It was New Year's Eve, December 31, 1990, and on the streets of Baghdad there was little talk of war. Thousands of revelers, dressed in their holiday finest, strolled idly along Saadoun Street, one of the capital's main thoroughfares. Army reservists on two-day leave from active duty popped in and out of the gaudy discotheques along the way. One group of bored young men stopped to watch a street brawl a block away from an Iraqi Airways office that had been car-bombed a few years earlier. Horns honked and people waved along the traffic-clogged street. Women in taffeta and ostrich feathers and furs, men in ill-fitting double-breasted suits, children in glittery costumes milled through the reception rooms of the al-Rasheed Hotel for a private party.

The lobby was still decorated with a scrawny Christmas tree and aluminum-foil garlands, and the public-address system played jazz renditions of well-worn Christmas carols. On the dance floor, couples swayed to popular Egyptian ballads. Liberation Square, where Jews and other "conspirators" were hanged as spies in 1969, was lit up with red and white lights like New York's Little Italy. Even the palm trees were strung with white and yellow lights. One façade of the Mansour Melia Hotel, which had been a way station for hundreds of foreign hostages until Saddam sent them all home a few weeks earlier, was festooned with blinking lights that greeted all of Baghdad with the words, *Happy New Year 1991.*

At the home of André Janier, the French chargé d'affaires, diplomats and foreign journalists gathered for the most elegant dinner party in town. Flouting the global embargo against Saddam, the Janiers had smuggled in from Paris six suitcases of delicacies—foie gras, white sausages, smoked salmon, turkeys, and the ingredients for nine desserts—accompanied by French champagne and wines. A French television crew filmed the evening's highlights for broadcast back home. Joseph C. Wilson IV, the American chargé d'affaires, danced with the Italian correspondent from *La Repubblica.* There were no Iraqis at the party. At the Foreign Ministry, meanwhile, Nizar Hamdoon, a deputy foreign minister and former ambassador to Washington [D.C.], sat in his office and watched a recap of the events of 1990 on Cable News Network (CNN). Eventually, even he left for a party at a private club.

> Saddam, under moonlight, stirred a huge pot of stew on a campfire. He poured liberal amounts of salt into the bubbling pot.

Saddam [Hussein] spent New Year's Eve with his commanders in Kuwait, or so the official Iraqi news media said. Dressed in a military overcoat and beret, a green silk scarf around his neck, the Iraqi leader was shown on television praying with his troops and kissing his officers on both cheeks. A commentator announced that Saddam had gone to the front to prepare dinner for his troops. With Bach's Brandenburg Concertos on the soundtrack, the television footage showed a flat, open field at an undisclosed location, where Saddam, under moonlight, stirred a huge pot of stew on a campfire. He poured liberal amounts of salt into the bubbling pot and showed some of his commanders how to stir it. After sampling the meal, he smiled broadly and shook the hands of Republican Guards who lined up for a brief—perhaps their last—encounter with their leader.

"We asked ourselves where we should go this night," he said to them. "The best place is with our armed forces." Then he launched into a 30-minute lecture, using the Islamic imagery that he adopted after his invasion of Kuwait, telling his men that the New Year would mark the "beginning of the hot confrontation between the alliance of believers . . . and the alliance of infidels, deviationists, and hypocrites." Saddam did not intend to miss an opportunity to remind his troops of their ancient greatness. They might be facing great adversity, he told

them, but they must not forget that Iraq was civilized 6,000 years ago, "when others were living in caves like beasts." They would triumph over the so-called superior Western technology, which was, after all, based "on Arab knowledge," he added.

Festivities Mask Desperation

On the surface, Baghdad was deceptively normal. Physically, the capital was not prepared for war. Although some shopkeepers taped their windows to prevent flying glass, few antiaircraft guns and no sandbags were visible. But beneath the calm was quiet desperation. On the morning of New Year's Day, the nation was suffering a collective hangover as the countdown to war began. The streets of Baghdad were empty, the storefronts shut tight. Iraqis wealthy enough to have basements had filled them with at least a month's supply of food and water. Thousands of others put their belongings on the roofs of their cars and fled the capital for indefinite visits to relatives in the countryside. Others settled in Najaf and Karbala, assuming that the American-led coalition would not bomb the holiest sites of Shiite Islam. A ban on all foreign travel left the Iraqi people no other choice.

Ordinary citizens vacillated between a confident belief that both sides were bluffing to a grim fatalism that the country would be plunged into another senseless war. They did not describe the crisis as a struggle for the liberation of Palestine or Arab glory. Yes, they said, they believed that Kuwait was a part of Iraq, but they spoke about it as an abstract fact that they had memorized in geography class as children, not as a burning political issue. Like their president, they were caught between the gloomy predictions emanating from Washington and their own wishful thinking. The United States wouldn't attack them, they said, a question in their voices. There would be a compromise at the last moment, wouldn't there? And even if there were an attack, how could it be

Photo on previous page: Despite the slide into economic distress, markets in Baghdad were filled with luxury goods beyond the reach of average Iraqis as the Gulf War began. (Roger Viollet/Getty Images.)

> "Most disheartened were Iraq's young men, many of them reservists who had fought in the war against Iran and wanted to get on with their lives."

worse than the eight years of suffering in the war with Iran? The city's mood seemed to shift with each bit of news. When Iraqi Foreign Minister Tariq Aziz agreed on January 4, 1991, to meet with U.S. Secretary of State James A. Baker III in Geneva five days later, the spirits of ordinary Baghdadis seemed to rise. In what might have been interpreted as a sign of confidence among the business community, the prices of luxury goods in the bazaar in central Baghdad rose as well. When the talks collapsed, so did the spirit of the people and the bargaining power of the merchants.

Most disheartened were Iraq's young men, many of them reservists who had fought in the war against Iran and wanted to get on with their lives. In the stalled Iraqi economy, many of them had become taxi drivers, and they hung around the hotels of Baghdad like vultures, waiting for a foreigner to hire them for the day. One day in December, Baghdad Radio announced that all healthy males born in 1957 had to report to military registration centers, to be given a date to report to duty. A 33-year-old Iraqi driver whom I knew had been born in that year. He had served nine and a half years in the Army as a communications expert, most of them during the war with Iran, then had become a sales manager for an export construction firm. The only problem was that his firm did business in Kuwait, and when the Iraqis invaded, his job disappeared. He had no wife, no children, no prospects. Now he would have to go to war again.

In one sense, Iraq's looting of Kuwait after the invasion gave Baghdad the look of abundance. The Iraqis took spanking-new blue Mercedes buses looted from Kuwait and put them to use on the bus routes of Baghdad. The shops along Saadoun Street were clogged with booty: canned fruits and vegetables, processed meats and cheeses, British chocolates, Rolex watches, Giorgio Armani sportcoats and Bruno Magli shoes, Japanese VCRs, bottles of Coke that said, "Keep Kuwait tidy." But these items were hopelessly beyond the budgets of the average Iraqi consumer. The overflowing shops were painful reminders of what Iraqis could not afford.

On another level, Iraq began to take on the look and feel of a once-rich country that had come on hard times. The global embargo, imposed shortly after Iraq's invasion of Kuwait, ground down the spirit of the people. Beggars, who had always been swept off the streets with the morning garbage, were allowed to sit at intersections and ask—aggressively—for money. The price of two automobile tires jumped from 35 dinars in the summer of 1989 to 500 dinars by New Year's Day. When tires became scarce at any price, their theft from cars left on the street became common, a shock to Baghdadis who were accustomed to the strict law and order that accompanied the country's repression.

Daily Life Becomes Much Harder

Cars and trucks were sidelined because of a shortage of spare parts. Hundreds of factories were closed. Baghdadis waited in line for two hours to buy bread at subsidized rates. By New Year's Day, the country was suffering from severe food shortages, particularly of rice, sugar, milk, and flour. Food-rationing coupons bought 25 to 50 percent less merchandise than they did when the rationing system was introduced the previous September. The week before I arrived, government agents had moved through private foodstalls in Baghdad to confiscate scarce staples and put them on sale in the government-owned shops.

The Iraqi Museum, always a calm refuge from the turmoil outside, was closed, its 200,000-piece collection packed into metal crates and stored in bunkers, along with the "Great Mesopotamian Exhibition," a selection of the best of the collection, originally scheduled to tour six American cities as part of a blossoming cultural exchange.

One by one, the better restaurants, even the ones in hotels, began to run out of certain items and then to close. Stores filled with furniture and toys and kitchenware—goods from pre-embargo days—were open but empty of customers. It was hard to believe that this was the country that possessed the second-largest oil reserves in the world, a rich, fertile country watered by the Tigris and the Euphrates [rivers]. The luxury hotels in Baghdad, where Western and Japanese dealmakers once did business, were now filled with an odd mixture of foreign intermediaries and journalists, delegations of offbeat Muslim groups, and, to my surprise, Kuwaitis. At the al-Rasheed Hotel, a woman who said she was a Hungarian princess wandered the corridors wearing a diamond tiara and a diaphanous dress. Three neo-Nazi pilots in uniforms decorated with swastikas and portraits of Saddam professed their intention to go to the front to die for him. Salah Khalaf, the second-in-command of the Palestine Liberation Organization [PLO], lived there until he went back to the PLO headquarters in Tunis, where he was gunned down—possibly on Saddam's orders—on January 14.

> Three neo-Nazi pilots in uniforms decorated with swastikas and portraits of Saddam professed their intention to go to the front to die for him.

The regime did its utmost to nurture antiwar sentiment and raise support in the Islamic world. Foreign peace activists volunteered to become human shields at the front lines to prevent the onslaught of allied troops. Their "peace camp" was a desert spot in Iraq hundreds of miles from the border between the opposing armies, but for them it was a symbol of their protest. "The more people who are here, the less chance there will be that

Westerners will make war," insisted Hedwig Raskob, a psychotherapist from Munich. Instead, they became part of Saddam's propaganda machine. When one group of activists was taken to visit a farm outside Baghdad, the farmers burst into song—a war song. "Saddam, you are our leader," they sang, "and we are your willing soldiers." At a peace ceremony not far from Iraq's border with Saudi Arabia, two women were assigned to water a newly planted olive tree. But Iraqi authorities decided that an Iraqi soldier, his rifle on his shoulder, should do the watering. It was not what the peace activists had in mind.

Most intriguing was the status of the Kuwaitis. While thousands of them were imprisoned or executed by the Iraqis, others were left alone, for no apparent reason. They either drove nine hours from Kuwait City to Baghdad in their Mercedeses and minivans or flew north on nonstop Iraqi Airways flights. Some came to use the international phones that were cut off back home or to find relatives who were arrested in Kuwait and transported to Baghdad prisons. Other Kuwaitis took refuge in Baghdad hotel suites. Baghdad was cheaper than Riyadh [Saudi Arabia], Bahrain, even Cairo [Egypt], and it was easy to come and go to Kuwait when they pleased. Still others went on shopping sprees, filling up their vans with food, toys, clothes, and other consumer goods unavailable in Kuwait. Even though the Iraqi authorities had decreed that the Kuwaiti dinar was worth only one Iraqi dinar, a fraction of its former value, there was a strong black market in Kuwaiti currency in Baghdad. Kuwaiti money was worth ten times more in Baghdad than it was in Kuwait City.

Strangeness and Denial Persist

At the American Embassy, Wilson taped on his office door a picture of John Lennon flashing the peace symbol in front of the Statue of Liberty, and he sent a bottle of wine from his home state of California to Foreign Minister Tariq Aziz, a Christian, for the New Year. Every day the Baath Party bused in hundreds of Iraqi women to chant slogans of peace outside the embassy. The demonstrations were timed to coincide with Wilson's briefings for the news media. To show that there were no bad feelings, Saddam sent the embassy a Yule-log cake and a bouquet of purple flowers.

Only when the last-minute Baker-Aziz talks failed in Geneva did Iraqis begin to realize that the country was on the brink of a catastrophic war. Even then, there was denial, and hopes were raised anew when Saddam announced that the National Assembly would convene on the evening of January 13, two days before the United Nations deadline. But the rubber-stamp body voted 220-1 in favor of a resolution affirming Iraq's annexation of Kuwait and authorizing the use of force to defend it. The diplomatic community packed up and departed, leaving the Iraqi people to face the consequences of war alone. The British ambassador, Harold Walker, took his staff to Jordan in a caravan of Range Rovers. Richard Ellerkmann, the German ambassador, left without saying goodbye to either Iraqi officials or fellow diplomats. At the British Club, a haven for Westerners for more than 70 years, there was no longer anyone to play darts or billiards. At the Netherlands Embassy, the chief security guard hurriedly burned huge bales of classified documents in oil drums before the embassy finally closed its doors.

On the eve of war, there was a tense calm among the functionaries in Iraq's Ministry of Information. These were "new Iraqi men" who conformed to Saddam's vision of greatness; they were the ultimate loyalists and also the most closely watched, because they acted as guides, and watchdogs, for foreign journalists. Yet they were uneasy when they talked about war.

Abbas was one of these new Iraqi men. A man in his early thirties whose shirts were too tight for his broad belly, he was my guide during two trips to Iraq in 1983 and 1984. Married, with two young sons, he had been an English major at Baghdad University, where he graduated at the top of his class. He had served in the Iran-Iraq war but never had to use his gun. Like his country and his president, Abbas was isolated, turned inward. Although he had never studied English abroad, he was required to interpret for non-Arabic-speaking journalists. He didn't know words like *slum* or *synagogue*, but could speak for hours about the "Zionist entity" and "imperialist enslavement." We had never been friends. In fact, on my previous trips, we had had violent arguments over what I could and could not do.

I saw Abbas again in Baghdad in early 1991, a few days before war broke out. He had spent five years as a press attaché in Europe and had lost 30 pounds. He was now earning about $1,500 a month at the official conversion rate, a salary worth only $100 a month because of inflation and the rampant black market. He now owned a car and an apartment in a new residential neighborhood of Baghdad. Life could not have been better, but he was gloomy and quiet in the face of the impending war. He asked, hypothetically, about the possibility of studying English in the United States. In a small but telling indication that sanctions were working, he wrote down a long list of medicines he needed for his family and asked if I could smuggle them in. "Look at all this," he said, pointing to the opulence of the al-Rasheed Hotel, in frustration. We're not a Third World country. We could lose it all." A few days later, Abbas and his countrymen were plunged into war.

Why the United States Decided to Attack

George H.W. Bush

Speaking from the Oval Office of the White House at 9:01 P.M. on January 16, 1991, the US president announced that air attacks on Iraqi leader Saddam Hussein's forces had begun two hours before. Below, the full text of George H.W. Bush's address sets forth why a military attack was necessary and what it aimed to accomplish. The president also quotes four individuals in the US armed forces about why the war effort is essential to peace and freedom. George H.W. Bush was elected the forty-first president of the United States in 1988. His single term in office included serving as the commander in chief during the Persian Gulf War.

Photo on following page: US president George H.W. Bush addressed the nation on January 16, 1991, as allied military forces began to attack targets in Iraq and Kuwait. (Associated Press.)

Just two hours ago, allied air forces began an attack on military targets in Iraq and Kuwait. These attacks continue as I speak. Ground forces are not engaged.

SOURCE. George H.W. Bush, "Address to the Nation Announcing Allied Military Action in the Persian Gulf," January 16, 1991.

This conflict started August 2 [1990] when the dictator of Iraq invaded a small and helpless neighbor. Kuwait—a member of the Arab League and a member of the United Nations [UN]—was crushed; its people, brutalized. Five months ago, Saddam Hussein started this cruel war against Kuwait. Tonight, the battle has been joined. This military action, taken in accord with United Nations resolutions and with the consent of the United States Congress, follows months of constant and virtually endless diplomatic activity on the part of the United Nations, the United States, and many, many other countries. Arab leaders sought what became known as an Arab solution, only to conclude that Saddam Hussein was unwilling to leave Kuwait. Others traveled to Baghdad in a variety of efforts to restore peace and justice. Our Secretary of State, James Baker, held an historic meeting in Geneva, only to be totally rebuffed. This past weekend, in a last-ditch effort, the Secretary-General of the United Nations went to the Middle East with peace in his heart—his second such mission. And he came back from Baghdad with no progress at all in getting Saddam Hussein to withdraw from Kuwait.

Now the 28 countries with forces in the Gulf area have exhausted all reasonable efforts to reach a peaceful resolution—have no choice but to drive Saddam from Kuwait by force. We will not fail.

> "Saddam sought to add to the chemical weapons arsenal he now possesses, an infinitely more dangerous weapon of mass destruction—a nuclear weapon."

As I report to you, air attacks are underway against military targets in Iraq. We are determined to knock out Saddam Hussein's nuclear bomb potential. We will also destroy his chemical weapons facilities. Much of Saddam's artillery and tanks will be destroyed. Our operations are designed to best protect the lives of all the coalition forces by targeting Saddam's vast military arsenal. Initial reports from General [Norman] Schwarzkopf are that our operations are proceeding according to plan.

Our objectives are clear: Saddam Hussein's forces will leave Kuwait. The legitimate government of Kuwait will be restored to its rightful place, and Kuwait will once again be free. Iraq will eventually comply with all relevant United Nations resolutions, and then, when peace is restored, it is our hope that Iraq will live as a peaceful and cooperative member of the family of nations, thus enhancing the security and stability of the Gulf.

The World Could Wait No Longer

Some may ask: Why act now? Why not wait? The answer is clear: The world could wait no longer.

Sanctions, though having some effect, showed no signs of accomplishing their objective. Sanctions were tried for well over 5 months, and we and our allies concluded that sanctions alone would not force Saddam from Kuwait.

While the world waited, Saddam Hussein systematically raped, pillaged, and plundered a tiny nation, no threat to his own. He subjected the people of Kuwait to unspeakable atrocities—and among those maimed and murdered, innocent children.

While the world waited, Saddam sought to add to the chemical weapons arsenal he now possesses, an infinitely more dangerous weapon of mass destruction—a nuclear weapon. And while the world waited, while the world talked peace and withdrawal, Saddam Hussein dug in and moved massive forces into Kuwait.

While the world waited, while Saddam stalled, more damage was being done to the fragile economies of the Third World, emerging democracies of Eastern Europe, to the entire world, including to our own economy.

The United States, together with the United Nations, exhausted every means at our disposal to bring this crisis

Changing the World

Less than two months after announcing the start of the Persian Gulf War, President George H.W. Bush told a joint session of Congress how the war was won and what major challenges now needed addressing.

Those challenges to which the United States must commit, Bush said, were working with other nations and people for peace in the Middle East, controlling weapons of mass destruction, and fostering "economic development for the sake of peace and progress."

With the victory, Bush said, "we can see . . . the very real prospect of a new world order . . . a world in which freedom and respect for human rights find a home among all nations."

to a peaceful end. However, Saddam clearly felt that by stalling and threatening and defying the United Nations, he could weaken the forces arrayed against him.

While the world waited, Saddam Hussein met every overture of peace with open contempt. While the world prayed for peace, Saddam prepared for war.

I had hoped that when the United States Congress, in historic debate, took its resolute action, Saddam would realize he could not prevail and would move out of Kuwait in accord with the United Nations resolutions. He did not do that. Instead, he remained intransigent, certain that time was on his side. Saddam was warned over and over again to comply with the will of the United Nations: Leave Kuwait, or be driven out. Saddam has arrogantly rejected all warnings. Instead, he tried to make this a dispute between Iraq and the United States of America.

Well, he failed. Tonight, twenty-eight nations—countries from five continents, Europe and Asia, Africa, and the Arab League—have forces in the Gulf area standing shoulder to shoulder against Saddam Hussein. These countries had hoped the use of force could be avoided. Regrettably, we now believe that only force will make him leave.

> We have before us the opportunity to forge for ourselves and for future generations a new world order.

Prior to ordering our forces into battle, I instructed our military commanders to take every necessary step to prevail as quickly as possible, and with the greatest degree of protection possible for American and allied service men and women. I've told the American people before that this will not be another Vietnam, and I repeat this here tonight. Our troops will have the best possible support in the entire world, and they will not be asked to fight with one hand tied behind their back. I'm hopeful that this fighting will not go on for long and that casualties will be held to an absolute minimum.

This is an historic moment. We have in this past year made great progress in ending the long era of conflict and cold war. We have before us the opportunity to forge for ourselves and for future generations a new world order—a world where the rule of law, not the law of the jungle, governs the conduct of nations. When we are successful—and we will be—we have a real chance at this new world order, an order in which a credible United Nations can use its peacekeeping role to fulfill the promise and vision of the UN's founders.

The US Stands Up for Freedom

We have no argument with the people of Iraq. Indeed, for the innocents caught in this conflict, I pray for their safety. Our goal is not the conquest of Iraq. It is the liberation of Kuwait. It is my hope that somehow the Iraqi people can, even now, convince their dictator that he must lay down his arms, leave Kuwait, and let Iraq itself rejoin the family of peace-loving nations.

[British-American revolutionary] Thomas Paine wrote many years ago: "These are the times that try men's souls." Those well-known words are so very true today. But even as planes of the multinational forces attack Iraq, I prefer to think of peace, not war. I am convinced not only that we will prevail but that out of the horror of combat will come the recognition that no nation can stand against a world united, no nation will be permitted to brutally assault its neighbor.

No President can easily commit our sons and daughters to war. They are the Nation's finest. Ours is an all-volunteer force, magnificently trained, highly motivated. The troops know why they're there. And listen to what they say, for they've said it better than any President or Prime Minister ever could.

Listen to Hollywood Huddleston, Marine lance corporal. He says, "Let's free these people, so we can go home and be free again." And he's right. The terrible crimes and tortures committed by Saddam's henchmen against the innocent people of Kuwait are an affront to mankind and a challenge to the freedom of all.

Listen to one of our great officers out there, Marine Lieutenant General Walter Boomer. He said: "There are things worth fighting for. A world in which brutality and lawlessness are allowed to go unchecked isn't the kind of world we're going to want to live in."

Listen to Master Sergeant J.P. Kendall of the 82nd Airborne: "We're here for more than just the price of a gallon of gas. What we're doing is going to chart the future of the world for the next 100 years. It's better to deal with this guy now than five years from now."

And finally, we should all sit up and listen to Jackie Jones, an Army lieutenant, when she says, "If we let him get away with this, who knows what's going to be next?"

I have called upon Hollywood and Walter and J.P. and Jackie and all their courageous comrades-in-arms to do what must be done. Tonight, America and the world are deeply grateful to them and to their families. And let me say to everyone listening or watching tonight: When the troops we've sent in finish their work, I am determined to bring them home as soon as possible.

Tonight, as our forces fight, they and their families are in our prayers. May God bless each and every one of them, and the coalition forces at our side in the Gulf, and may He continue to bless our nation, the United States of America.

The Persian Gulf Region Was Highly Unstable and Militarized

Abdulkhaleq Abdulla

Iraq's invasion should have surprised no one familiar with the Persian Gulf region's history of conflict, according to the following viewpoint by an Arab specialist. Several factors contribute to the area's instability, Abdulkhaleq Abdulla writes, including immense oil reserves, a large number of dictatorial governments, and the conditions introduced by British colonialism. Saddam Hussein himself embodies the region's contradictions, ambitions, power impulses, and frustrations. In this particular war, though, the responsibility was entirely his own, Abdulla maintains. Abdulla is a political science professor at United Emirates University. He holds a doctorate from Georgetown University in Washington, D.C., and is the author of several books and numerous articles and reports on the Persian Gulf region.

SOURCE. Abdulkhaleq Abdulla, "Gulf War: The Socio-Political Background," *Arab Studies Quarterly*, vol. 16, no. 3, Summer 1994. Copyright © 1994 by Association of Arab-American University Graduates and Institute of Arab Studies. Reproduced by permission of *Arab Studies Quarterly*.

The Arab Gulf region has gone through two tragic wars in nearly one decade. The first war, between Iran and Iraq, which began in September 1980, lasted for eight long years. This war has been labeled by some as one of the costliest conflicts in the 20th Century, whereas others referred to it as the longest war. Two years after the cease-fire between Iran and Iraq, the latter, taking the whole world by surprise, invaded Kuwait. The shocking 2 August 1990 invasion set in motion a series of political, diplomatic and military activities which eventually led to the 16 January 1991 war. This second Gulf war lasted for only 42 days, but was nevertheless as damaging and as catastrophic as the first.

Many people in the Gulf thought that the Iran-Iraq War would be the last major war in this vital and sensitive region. The damages and the human suffering caused by the eight year war were thought to be enormous enough to convince the leaders of the Gulf states to avoid further wars and settle their legitimate differences and disputes peacefully. Most of these states were yearning for a peaceful and more tranquil 1990s. The people of the Gulf, too, were optimistic that the worst moment in recent memory was finally over, and they were looking for a new start. As it turned out, this was ill-founded optimism. "The war to liberate Kuwait" turned out to be also a war for the complete and total destruction of Iraq as a major Gulf power. . . .

The sociopolitical background to much of the tensions, conflicts and wars in the Gulf include some diverse factors such as: the long lasting colonial legacy, the 1971 British withdrawal, the unresolved border disputes, the existence of a number of vulnerable small states, the 1973 oil price increase, the ongoing international interest in oil, the strains of rapid modernization, the 1979 resignation of the Shah and the consolidation of a revolutionary Islamic Republic in Iran, the continuation of one-man, one-family, one-party regimes and finally the persistence of foreign meddling which only exacerbates local conflicts and easily transforms them into potentially deadly and catastrophic wars with vast global consequences. Each of these sociopolitical factors, which have a bearing on one another, is itself a sufficient source of conflict, but all of them combined have worked over the last 20 years to produce the last crisis and war in the Gulf.

Many Conflicts of Many Types

The Arab Gulf, composed of eight states that vary in size and importance, is characterized by two distinct political features. First, the Gulf is essentially a conflict oriented region. The states of the region have nearly always been in [a] state of conflict with each other. Throughout their modern history, these states have been engaged in all sorts of conflicts which have taken many different forms: tribal wars, border wars, oil wars and even political and ideological wars. Intra- and inter-state conflicts reoccur in the region on almost regular intervals. Of course, the discovery of oil in large quantity and the sudden international importance of Gulf oil has made the region even more volatile and conflict-oriented. Oil has made the newly independent small states super-affluent and financially secure, but it has also made them politically and militarily vulnerable and susceptible to all sons of external envies, involvements and even invasions. Hence, when it comes to the Gulf region, conflict is the rule whereas peaceful coexistence and cooperation is the rare exception.

> It seems hardly likely in the future that such an extremely oil rich and highly strategic region . . . would be free from outside influence and domination.

The other distinct political characteristic of this region is that the Gulf is essentially an other-directed regional system. This region, probably more than any other, has been guided by outward influences rather than those from within. The Gulf regional system either lacks inner dynamism and direction, or else its inner dynamism has been historically suppressed by external necessities. In the first place, the Gulf is geographically, politically and culturally a subsystem of the wider Arab World-Middle East system which directly determines much of its politics. But the Gulf region is also probably one of the most financially and commercially integrated regions in the world capitalist system. This system exercises near total hegemony over the Gulf's economic choices and developmental strategies. Even after formal political independence, the states of the Gulf never had the chance to freely manage their own affairs and assert indigenous control over Gulf politics and economics. It seems hardly likely in the future that such an extremely oil rich and highly strategic region like the Gulf would be free from outside influence and domination. Hence, when it comes to the Gulf, it is safe to generalize that foreign involvement and control is the rule whereas indigenous-local management of Gulf affairs is the distinct exception.

The last two wars, and especially the vast global interest in the invasion of Kuwait, certainly confirm these two fundamental political rules of the Gulf region. The two wars were merely one more manifestation of the tense and conflictual characteristic of this region. The tragic events and consequences of the last Gulf war have in turn contributed to the region's inherent instability, volatility and fragility. The destruction and suffering, which are unmatched in recent memory, have made the Gulf sad, depressed and indeed more insecure than ever before. On the other hand, the massive and unprecedented direct foreign military participation in the second Gulf war reinforces the other-directedness of the region. This last war was primarily viewed and justified as essential not just to liberating Kuwait and securing peace in the Gulf, but as a necessary element to the building of the so-called New World Order. In his January 1991 State of the Union address, President [George H.W.] Bush declared that what is at stake is a New World Order. However, it is questionable that the New World Order, however real, and the presence of foreign troops, of whatever nationality, would lessen tensions, prevent future wars or make the Gulf more stable. . . .

British Power Sets the Stage

The starting point for most of the contemporary issues in the Gulf is the 1971 British withdrawal and the British colonial legacy in the Gulf. For nearly 150 years, Britain was the sole power in the area. It unilaterally and systematically altered the political and geographic realities in the region. It changed rules, created new states, imposed artificial borders and basically preserved the backwardness and traditionality of the existing tribal order. Many of these realities, created by the colonial power, continue to exist and decisively influence and shape contemporary developments. When Britain decided to remove its direct military presence in the area, it left behind a power vacuum and a number of vulnerable newly independent small states that also happened to be oil rich. Gulf security became an instant political problem which has never been settled. Who would guard this strategically valuable region? The Shah of Iran, aided and promoted by the United States, attempted to assert his domination throughout much of the 1970s. This was naturally resented and challenged by many Arabs, particularly by Iraq, which emerged by the late 1980s as the dominant regional power with enhanced capabilities and a desire to influence events in the Gulf including oil price and production.

The 1973 oil price increase immediately transformed the Gulf into one of the most sensitive regions in the world. The Gulf and particularly Gulf oil became the center of global interests. More oil is to be found in the

Photo on following page: Iraqi president Saddam Hussein was a dictator in a region that felt deep anger toward the West and a common humiliation over the failure to unify all Arabs in a single unit. (Time & Life Pictures/Getty Images.)

region than anywhere else in the world, and while oil reserves everywhere are decreasing, Gulf oil reserves, on the other hand, increase daily. Furthermore, more countries are using oil today than ever before and all of them are becoming more and more dependent on Gulf oil. Oil, and especially Gulf oil, remain the motivating force of industrial society and the lifeblood of the civilization that it helped create. It is still the basis for the world's biggest business, one that embodies the extremes of risk and reward, as well as the interplay and conflict between entrepreneurship and corporate enterprise, and between private business and the nation-state. It also remains—as demonstrated during the Gulf war—an essential element in national power, a major factor in world economies, a critical focus for war and conflict and a decisive force in international affairs. It is these oil facts that have made the Gulf an internationally significant place since 1973. They will also make it even more significant in the years ahead.

> Oil nearly always plays some role in the constant reoccurring of conflicts, tensions and wars in the region.

Oil's global significance is, of course, a source of some joy to the states in the Gulf, but it is also making many of them vulnerable and exposed to all sorts of external influences. Since 1973, oil has become the key determining factor for all development in the region. Oil nearly always plays some role in the constant reoccurring of conflicts, tensions and wars in the region. It is responsible for initiating conflicts, exacerbating and prolonging them and most often transforming purely domestic tension into a crisis of profound global consequence. The last Gulf war is undoubtedly a prime example. This war was fundamentally an oil war. Oil was at stake, and when oil is at stake, all the talk of international legality and cooperation and world peace and order sound somewhat disingenuous.

Oil became even more internationally significant in 1979 after the unexpected downfall of the Shah, the protector of Western interests in the region. The emergence and the gradual consolidation of the revolutionary Islamic republic in Iran represented an unwanted challenge to the status quo in the Gulf. The outbreak of the Iran-Iraq war was one attempt to contain and defeat Islamic radicalism in Iran. Iraq, in essence, fought for eight years a proxy war to contain revolutionary Iran and preserve the status quo which best benefitted Western interests and objectives. Iraq, aided and supported by the West and the Arab Gulf states, was successful. It emerged as the undisputed political and military regional power but was also financially and economically weak. This combination of military strength and economic impotence invariably breeds foreign adventure such as Iraq's reckless invasion of Kuwait.

This Is a Region of Dictators

The Arab Gulf region is, of course, full of oil, but this region is also full of dictatorial and authoritarian regimes. There are probably more one-man, one-family political systems in the Gulf than in any other comparably small geographic location in the world. The region is virtually saturated with medieval and traditional rulers who enjoy absolute non-constitutional power that can make or break a whole nation. Oil, while triggering rapid socio-economic transformation, has, ironically enough, prevented meaningful political change. It has led to political rigidity and absolutist power being given to one-man, one-party or else one-family in the society. It is these contemporary political realities, i.e. the lack of democracy, and the lack of political participation that are the root cause of much of the tensions in the Gulf today.

The war in the Gulf was the product of a number of highly regrettable decisions taken by the rulers of Kuwait, Saudi Arabia and Iraq. The ruling family in Kuwait

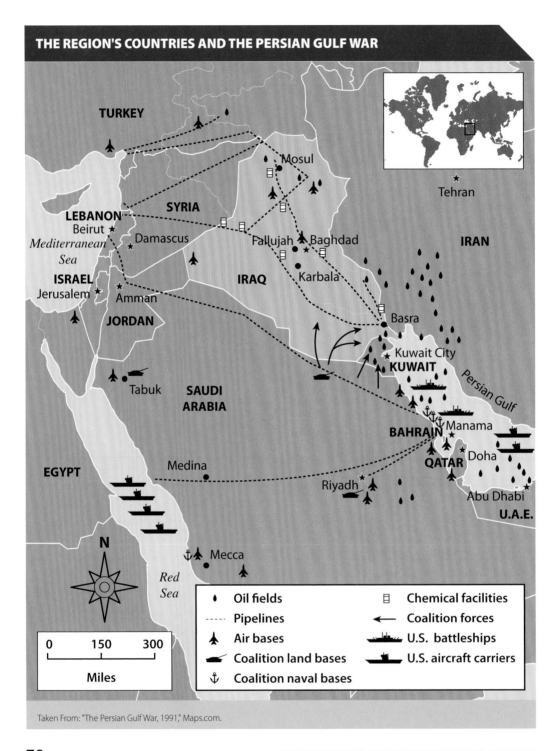

THE REGION'S COUNTRIES AND THE PERSIAN GULF WAR

TURKEY

Mosul

Tehran

SYRIA

LEBANON
Beirut ★
Mediterranean Damascus
Sea

Fallujah ★ Baghdad

IRAN

ISRAEL
Jerusalem ★

Karbala

IRAQ

Amman

Basra

JORDAN

Kuwait City
KUWAIT

Tabuk

SAUDI
ARABIA

Persian Gulf

BAHRAIN Manama

EGYPT

Medina

QATAR Doha

Riyadh

Abu Dhabi

U.A.E.

N

*Red
Sea*

Mecca

● Oil fields		▯ Chemical facilities
----- Pipelines		← Coalition forces
♠ Air bases		▅ U.S. battleships
◣ Coalition land bases		◣ U.S. aircraft carriers
⚓ Coalition naval bases		

0   150   300

Miles

Taken From: "The Persian Gulf War, 1991," Maps.com.

mismanaged its relationship with Iraq prior to August 1991. On the other hand, Saddam Hussein's unjustified decision to invade Kuwait was an outrageous violation of international legality and the principle of self-determination. Finally, it was the Saudi ruling family's decision to invite American troops that made war more likely. These three interrelated decisions are equally responsible for the initiation of the war and for much of the current political polarization in the Arab World. These decisions are the natural products of a lack of democracy and the prevalence of highly centralized politics in these states.

> "President Hussein belongs to an Arab World which is full of unrealized dreams, full of unresolved disputes and full of uncertainties and frustrations."

Saddam Hussein embodies the ultimate centralization and personalization of power and authority. He is the central figure in the last Gulf crisis and immensely contributed to the making of the war. Mr. Hussein is, indeed, a highly complex leader. He is a typical Machiavellian [cunning] leader who conspicuously enjoys power and authority and does not tolerate any challenge to his leadership. But he is also a product of a peculiar historical and regional circumstance. President Hussein belongs to an Arab World which is full of unrealized dreams, full of unresolved disputes and full of uncertainties and frustrations. He, like many other ordinary Arabs, feels deeply humiliated because the Arab World has not been able to unite, to develop and above all has been unable to liberate Palestine. It is probably these unrealized pan-Arab issues that contribute to Hussein's and other Arab leaders occasional rage against Western domination in the region.

The last war in the Gulf was above all Saddam Hussein's war. He decided to invade Kuwait, he played the brinkmanship game, he misread the political realities of the New World Order, he over-estimated his military capabilities and certainly underestimated American military might and its determination to use force. It was he who initiated this conflict and insisted on the war and he alone deserves the humiliation and the agony of defeat. The ultimate lesson for him and other Arabs is not so much that one-man rule is dangerous (which it is). Rather, it is that in the conduct of any conflict, what matters is how leaders conceptualize its nature and anticipate its course, on the basis of their specific understanding of both friends and foes, whether military, economic or political.

CHAPTER 2

Controversies Surrounding the Persian Gulf War

The War Was Absolutely Justifiable

James Turner Johnson

The following viewpoint outlines the seven criteria traditionally used to determine whether military force is justifiable, and finds that the Persian Gulf War clearly qualified. The author concludes there was a good reason to fight Iraq, the force that did so was morally based, the campaign was carried out with the right intentions, the goal was peace, the results outweighed the fighting's harm, a good outcome was likely, and measures short of war would not have succeeded. James Turner Johnson has been a professor of religion and university director of international programs at Rutgers University. He has written and edited numerous books, including *Can Modern War Be Just?*

SOURCE. James Turner Johnson, "The Just War Tradition and the American Military," *Just War and the Gulf War*, edited by James Turner Johnson and George Weigel. Copyright © 1991 by the Ethics and Public Policy Center. All rights reserved. Reproduced by permission of James Turner Johnson.

The just war tradition has arrived at seven criteria that must be satisfied to justify resorting to military force. These include just cause, right authority for the use of such force, right intention, the goal of restoring peace, overall proportionality of good over evil, a reasonable hope of success, and a situation of last resort. I will define each criterion more fully, and then examine each in the context of the decision to use force against Iraq.

What Just Cause Means

Just cause classically included one or more of three conditions: defense against an attack, recovery of something wrongly taken, or punishment of evil. These terms derive from Roman law and practice and were incorporated into the developing Christian moral theory of justified war by Saint Augustine in the early fifth century. In the Middle Ages the idea of punishment of evil was stressed by thinkers like Thomas Aquinas, who cited as their warrant Romans 13:4: "For [the prince] does not bear the sword in vain; he is the servant of God to execute his wrath on the evildoer."

In order to avoid defining evil in ideological terms, recent just war theorists have tended to focus on one particular evil, the aggressive use of force by a people or nation against another. There has been a corresponding tendency to emphasize defense against ongoing or imminent attack as the primary or only just cause for resort to force. This is clearly the case in contemporary international law, as provided in Articles 2 and 51 of the United Nations [UN] Charter. Yet it should not be thought that the earlier notions—of recovery of something wrongly taken, and punishment of evil—have evaporated from the tradi-

> [Iraq's action against Kuwait] was a flagrant case of aggression, one that violated the most fundamental norms of international order.

tion; rather, they have been subsumed within a gradually broadened concept of defense that allows retaliation for an attack launched and completed (punishment of evil) and defines wrongful occupation of territory as a state of "continuing" armed attack.

When Iraq invaded Kuwait on August 2, 1990, and declared that the territory that was "formerly Kuwait" was "irrevocably" part of Iraq, a just cause for use of force against Iraq came into being. This was a flagrant case of aggression, one that violated the most fundamental norms of international order, and it was quickly recognized as such by the United States, by the United Nations Security Council, and also by the overwhelming majority of nations of the world. Not only did Iraq's action blatantly violate the letter of Article 2 of the U.N. Charter (prohibiting "use of force against the territorial integrity [and] political independence" of another country), but, more profoundly, it showed utter disregard for the very norm on which the state system, and through it the United Nations itself, stands: a *de facto* acceptance of every state's right to exist.

The presence of just cause alone is not sufficient to justify resort to force; yet this was as clear and unambiguous a case as one could hope to find in the real world, and the brazenness of Iraq's action remained on public display even as the international community tried to expel the Iraqis through a variety of non-military means.

Critics of the use of force against Iraq cited as (at least partial) justification of Iraq's action various forms of "aggression" employed by Kuwait against Iraq: notably, keeping oil prices lower than was advantageous to Iraq and allegedly pumping oil from Iraqi territory by horizontal drilling. Even if these charges were true, such actions clearly fell far short of the magnitude necessary to justify military retaliation. Rather, conflicts of this sort are to be dealt with by negotiation and arbitration; that is what the very idea of a "world order" conveys.

Right Authority Has a Moral Basis

The second criterion for justified use of force is that such action be undertaken by a *right authority*. In historical terms, this meant a genuinely sovereign prince, that is, one with no political superior. In its early development, the principal function of this criterion was to limit the use of force to those who would rightly employ it, declaring illegitimate any use of force by subordinate nobles, private soldiers, criminals, and even the church. In the modern period the criterion of right authority still seeks to minimize the frequency of resort to force, by limiting it to the political leadership of a sovereign state duly authorized by the legitimate political processes of that state. (The concept of such authority has been extended also to the U.N. Security Council under the conditions specified in the Charter.)

A shop owner stands in front of his former jewelry store, destroyed in the aftermath of the Persian Gulf War. In the just-war tradition, Iraq's aggression toward Kuwait warranted US retaliation under the theory of "proportionality." (**Associated Press.**)

In the case of the Gulf War, right authority for use of force by the coalition of nations cooperating to undo Iraq's aggression was manifest at both the international and national levels. Internationally, such authority was provided by Resolution 678 of the United Nations Security Council. Within the United States, right authority derived first from the president's powers as defined by the Constitution and the War Powers Act, then by the congressional resolutions adopted on January 12 and 13 [1991] authorizing use of U.S. military force against Iraq.

Underlying such legal authority is a moral basis for the notion that right authority may use force to serve justice in the international arena. That moral claim is expressed in the same biblical passage, Romans 13:4, that medieval theorists cited to define the idea of justified cause. This passage also embodies an understanding that persons in positions of political authority have a responsibility to uphold the moral order as such, for without it human community would not be possible. This responsibility is not specifically religious or Western—though it is clearly present both in biblical religion and in the political traditions on which Western societies are founded—but is rather a universal concept, the basis of the idea of "world order" that undergirds international law and the United Nations system. Even if it were exclusively religious or Western, this concept of the responsibilities stemming from legitimate political authority would still impose a moral obligation on the political leadership of the American people and on the American people themselves.

> In the Middle Ages . . . soldiers were obligated to do penance after battle in case they had fought with forbidden motivations in their hearts.

Right Intention Has Two Sides

Right intention, the third notion bearing on the just war decision to resort to force, was classically defined in two ways: positively, by considering whether the other just war criteria were present; and negatively, by distinguishing itself from *wrong* intentions such as those enumerated by Augustine: "the love of violence, revengeful cruelty, fierce and implacable enmity, wild resistance and the lust for power, and such like." In the Middle Ages the requirement of right intention was taken especially seriously as a duty for individuals in combat; soldiers were obligated to do penance after battle in case they had fought with forbidden motivations in their hearts. In the modern period the concept of right intention has become a matter of the conduct of states, not the moral attitudes of individuals. It centers, positively, on such goals as protection or restoration of national, civil, and human rights and other values, reestablishment of order and stability, and the promotion of peace. Negatively, right intention today involves avoiding taking another state's territory, violating the rights of individuals or nations, and deliberately depriving a nation of peace and stability.

All these conditions existed when the United States and allied forces decided to take military action against Iraq. While critics sought to portray U.S. involvement in terms of "blood for oil" or as an effort to secure American hegemony in the Gulf region, such charges ignore the naked act of military aggression (and not the first such act on the part of Iraq) that brought the conflict into being. These critics also assumed bad faith on the part of U.S. and coalition leaders who insisted that their goals were simply to restore Kuwait as a nation and to require Iraq to make amends for damage it caused. Clearly, the subsequent military operation by coalition forces kept to these goals. Indeed, so off-base were the critics in depicting larger motives that, looking back on the internal bloodbath and repression that has swept over Iraq after the international cease-fire, one may wonder whether a broader "right intention" might not, in fact, have been justified: deposition of the dictator Saddam Hussein and

The Feminine Touch

Would war be more just if women had more of a stake in it? The question has yet to be answered in reality because such a small proportion of fighting forces have been made up of women.

On the US side in the Persian Gulf, though, about 35,000 women participated, with a dozen of them being killed, according to an article in *The Bulletin of the Atomic Scientists*. The article noted a *USA Today* report quoting Congresswoman Pat Schroeder of Colorado saying that all who served in the Persian Gulf were in essence in combat. "The realities of modern warfare make it difficult to define a field of battle," Schroeder said. "Military personnel, regardless of their position, are likely to be exposed to danger."

A case against women making ethical changes in the battlefield was put by retired Marine general Robert H. Barrow in the *New York Times*: "Combat is . . . killing. It's uncivilized. And women can't do it."

creation of the conditions for participatory government in Iraq as a way of serving the human and political rights of the Iraqi people.

Order, Justice, and Peace Go Together

The existence of a right intention on the part of the coalition in this case also substantially satisfied the requirement that the use of force *aim at achieving peace*. This criterion was understood classically in terms of three values: order, justice, and peace. The first aim of good politics, according to this view, is an order that reflects the natural law, that is, one that establishes things the way they *ought* to be. This would lead naturally to the existence of justice: a good order is inherently a just one, and maintaining justice protects the right ordering of affairs and relationships within the political community. The establishment of order and justice together produces the third political goal: peace. Peace would flow not only from the right ordering of politics within a society, but from the creation or restoration of a just political order in the relationships within, between, and among nations.

In the case of the Gulf War, the goal of peace was closely tied to the concept of right intention: rolling back Iraqi aggression and restoring Kuwaiti territory and sovereignty (right order and justice), deterring such aggression in the future, restoring the shattered peace of the region, and attempting to set in place safeguards to protect that peace in the future. I will return to this subject later on. What received too little attention, as we can see in retrospect, was the need to establish a just political order internally within Iraq as a key part of securing peace in the Gulf region. Given the focus of international law on affairs *between* nations, however, and the reluctance of the international community (including the coalition partners) to interfere in the internal affairs of nations, it is understandable that the coalition confined its conception of post-crisis peace to the restoration of order among the affected nations. The broader just war tradition differs from international law on this matter of whether the use of force to achieve peace should extend to efforts to produce the conditions of peace within the offending state; the moral argument imposes a more extensive responsibility than the legal. . . .

Good Results Must Clearly Outweigh Evil

The next just war concept to be examined is the criterion of *proportionality*, which refers to the effort to calculate the overall balance of good versus evil in deciding whether to use force to right a wrong. One must first assess the evil that has already been done—damage to

> Critics of the use of force vastly overestimated the expected costs of war.

lives and property, as well as harm to the more intangible values of human rights, self-government, and a peaceful and stable world order. Second, one must calculate the costs of allowing the situation of wrongdoing to continue. Finally, one must evaluate the various means of righting these wrongs in terms of their own costs, as well as the benefits they might produce.

In the debate that took place over U.S. participation in the United Nations-sanctioned use of force against Iraq, the just war criterion of proportionality was widely misapplied. Critics of the use of force vastly overestimated the expected costs of war while paying little attention to the damage already done, and continuing to be done, by Iraq's aggression against Kuwait. For these critics, the moral problem was not Iraq's actions but the American military buildup, which they deemed "disproportionate." The decision whether to take military action requires a much more inclusive and objective weighing of good versus ill.

The calculation of proportionality must take into account the many levels of force that responsible leaders may choose. While there may be occasions in which a buildup would serve as an effective deterrent, there are numerous other ways of engaging in combat, each carrying its own costs and benefits.

Applying the criterion of proportionality is properly an exercise in moral and political judgment, not a mathematical calculation. While it is easy to count military personnel, tanks, airplanes, and munitions, it is more difficult to agree on the value that should be placed on protection of human rights, national territorial and governmental integrity, and other such intangibles. Yet these are among the paramount values the just war tradition seeks to preserve, and their importance is undeniable. Equally undeniable is the fact that different peoples and cultures place different stock in these values. For this reason, governments need to take special care when invoking considerations of proportionality to keep from conceiving the issue in narrowly political or cultural terms.

A Good Outcome Must Be Likely

The decision to resort to force, to be justified, must also rest on a conviction that military action will have a *reasonable hope of success*. Clearly this, too, is a matter for prudential judgment, since "success" can be interpreted in many ways. While the fundamental goal of just war tradition is the protection and preservation of values—specifically, the establishment of right order, justice, and peace, within this broad context any particular just use of force may have its own specific aims. Indeed, such aims are inherently narrower than the overarching goal of right politics, a goal that is achieved by many instruments, only one of which is the justified use of force.

The use of force may establish the *conditions* for order, justice, and peace by eliminating the threats posed to them; that is the most realistic definition of "success" in the use of military force. The actual *achievement* of these goals is the broader work of good statecraft, building on the base of the established conditions. [Soldier and military theorist Carl Philipp Gottlieb von] Clausewitz's famous dictum, "War is the continuation of politics by other means," has a corollary: it is the business of politics to build on what a just war makes possible. A justified resort to force will have a "reasonable hope of success" if it lays the groundwork for productive statecraft (or, at the minimum, does not foster a situation that might make such statecraft impossible).

It is inappropriate to demand that a just use of force achieve ends beyond its means. This is why, in both classic and contemporary just war reasoning, the idea of specific and limited war goals is central. It is also why just war tradition developed a *ius in bello*—a set of restraints on what may morally be done when fighting a justified war. The concept of *ius in bello* involves more than insuring that the means of war are justifiable in themselves; it also involves establishing a correct relationship between the belligerents, both during the war and afterwards, since it recognizes that the existence of such a relationship is an important precondition for the creation of a just and lasting peace. "Reasonable hope of success," then, turns on the understanding of just cause and right intention, and includes not only achieving the goals thus established but also observing the limits on means laid out in the *ius in bello*. What is called for, in short, is a reasonable hope of doing what is justified by these moral criteria within the moral limits they define.

War Is the Last Resort

Finally, before engaging in military action, a government should determine whether the wrongs involved can be redressed by means other than force. It is important to note that the criterion of last resort does not mean that all possible non-military options that may be conceived of must first be tried; rather, a prudential judgment must be made as to whether *only* a rightly authorized use of force can, in the given circumstances, achieve the goods defined by the ideas of just cause, right intention, and the goal of peace, at a proportionate cost, and with reasonable hope of success. Other methods *may* be tried first, if time permits and if they also satisfy these moral criteria; yet this is not mandated by the criterion of last resort—and "last resort" certainly does not mean that other methods must be tried indefinitely.

It is my judgment that all the just war criteria providing guidance on the justified use of force were amply satisfied in the case of the decision to use military force against Iraq. The decision not to continue with negotiations or economic sanctions after January 15, 1991, did not violate the criterion of "last resort." The failure of the Geneva talks, the continued intransigence of Saddam Hussein, the ongoing process of military buildup by Iraqi forces, the continuing systematic rape of Kuwait, the history of Iraq's relations with its own dissident population and its neighbors, and threats of violence by Iraq against those neighbors all provided ample reasons to conclude that non-military means held little possibility of success, and that the continuing atrocities in Kuwait necessitated action.

Indeed, Iraq was an easy case. Most instances are fraught with much more ambiguity. There was no moral equivalence between Iraq and Kuwait, for example, or between Iraq and the coalition nations. Iraq's actions flagrantly violated both international law and the deeper international conscience expressed in the idea of a peaceful and stable world order. Nor were military forces committed by the United States or the other coalition nations behind closed doors; the authorization was public, was worked out in debate, and, when it came, clearly represented the will of the authorizing bodies. The critics' charges of a hidden American agenda were not borne out, either during or after the fact. The use of force was proportionate, given the wrongs that were to be righted. The continual aggression on the part of Saddam Hussein swept away, one by one, other possible means of resolving the crisis short of force. The judgment of a reasonable hope of success was eminently sound. The coalition's military action was motivated by the desire to lay a foundation for peace. While the final establishment of peace in the Gulf region and throughout the Middle East clearly remains to be accomplished, that is the proper task for statecraft, and exceeds the bounds of what military force alone can ever achieve.

The War Was an Unjustifiable Exercise of Arrogance

Alan Geyer and Barbara G. Green

The US-led coalition rushed to war without giving peaceful alternatives a real chance to work, according to Alan Geyer and Barbara G. Green in the following viewpoint. In particular, the United Nations sanctions against Iraq were not pursued sufficiently. Instead, the authors say, vengeance was an overriding motive, contrary to the precept that justice is found in the love and mercy of God. The tradition of "just war" was abused, civilians suffered greatly, and the future security of all nations was ill-served, they write. Alan Geyer is an author, a professor of political ethics at Wesley Theological Seminary, and a senior scholar at the Churches' Center for Theology and Public Policy. Barbara G. Green has been associate for peacemaking issues in the Washington, D.C., office of the Presbyterian Church (U.S.A.).

SOURCE. Alan Geyer and Barbara G. Green, "Toward a Just Peace," *Lines in the Sand: Justice and the Gulf War.* Copyright © 1992 by Alan Francis Geyer and Barbara Graham Green. Used by permission of Westminster John Knox Press. www.wjkbooks.com.

At the outset of this case study, we suggested that the just war tradition offers a useful checklist of significant moral questions concerning both the resort to war and the actual conduct of war. The conspicuous citation of that tradition in public rhetoric during the Gulf conflict of 1990–91 persuaded us that the moral issues of the war could be illuminated, at least in part, by using the tradition's concepts as a framework for our analysis.

But we also indicated at the beginning that the fullness of justice is too often obscured, not only by the misuse and abuse of the just war tradition but by the limitations of the tradition itself.

A truly foundational ethic of war and peace must begin by taking the fullest possible account of the moral burdens of history that weigh upon any conflict between and among nations. Because historical responsibility for the causes of conflict typically is shared, a keen sense of the ambiguities of justice will help prepare conflicting nations for every prospect of peaceful settlement. Such a sense is spiritually nurtured especially by acknowledging the necessity of repentance as the precondition of reconciliation. The incapacity of nations and their leaders to admit even the possibility of repentance is often more a sign of weakness than of some real strength beneath their proud belligerence. That incapacity may also reflect profound historical ignorance or forgetfulness.

An adequate ethic of war and peace will not be totally preoccupied by the presumed evils of aggressive violence, whether border-crossings or insurrections. Too often the nations or groups perpetrating such acts have themselves been victimized by long histories of systemic violence in the form of economic exploitation, racial brutality, and political tyranny. Those who go to war against the victims of imperial and institutional oppression never have a monopoly on justice.

This So-Called Just War Devastated Civilians

The justification of warfare and weaponry in terms of the traditional distinction between military and civilian targets has lost much of its presumed clarity. Modern military technology is produced by intricate complexes of government bureaucracies, arms industries, research institutions, power plants, and communications and transportation systems: complexes that intimately mesh military activities with most other social institutions, even with basic infrastructures. From a strategic perspective, therefore, it may seem necessary for bombs and missiles to attack an unlimited range of targets throughout a society's institutional fabric. But the direct and indirect civilian casualties and devastation from such warfare (as was the case in U.S.-Coalition warfare against Iraq) make invocations of the traditional norms of just conduct increasingly fatuous.

The traditional preoccupation with an *ethic of intention* to distinguish between military and civilian targets must yield to a much more consequential ethic that knows how indiscriminately destructive and deadly warfare has become—an *ethic that therefore strengthens the presumption against any resort to war*. The "collateral damage" done by either conventional or unconventional weapons can scarcely be justified any longer by the traditional claim of "double effect," that is, that such "damage" is the unintended consequence of military action. No consequence of the Gulf War is more dangerous or more perverse than the pretentious assumption that the presumed "success" and "morality" of the U.S.-Coalition assault on Iraq have, once again, made the resort to war an acceptable option or even a paradigm for the future of military policy.

The possession of overwhelming military force by a great power makes genuinely multilateral institutions of

> The moral pretenses to universalism by a great power can be among the most demonic forces of history.

peacemaking and peacekeeping more important, not less so, lest the great power presume police authority to intervene in conflicts anywhere in the world. Multilateral institutions acting within a framework of common security potentially offer more effective instruments for crisis intervention, war prevention, and military restraint than the "might makes right" presumptions of a great power.

What is particularly perilous—witness the Gulf War—is a great power's pressuring an international organization for a global license to decide unilaterally whether, when, how, and to what extremes to wage war. The moral pretenses to universalism by a great power can be among the most demonic forces of history. Essentially unilateral warfare tends, much more than do

A charred body is discovered after an allied bombing in Iraq's Amiriya district killed 500 women and children. (Getty Images.)

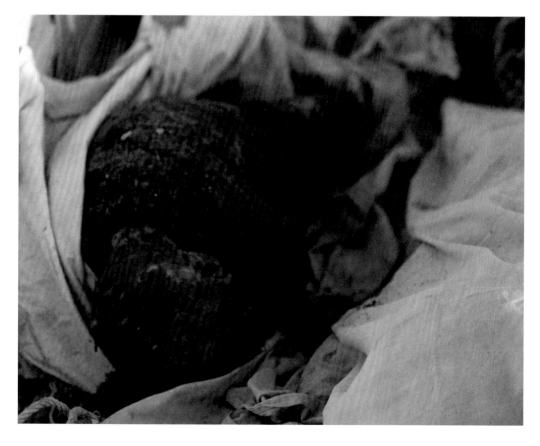

international organizations, to make use of hate images, untruthful propaganda, and spurious appeals to patriotism—all of which intensify hostilities and make peaceful settlement especially difficult.

Another particularly grievous legacy of the Gulf crisis is the unilateral U.S. decision to abandon primary reliance on economic sanctions. Those sanctions offered one of history's most promising opportunities to demonstrate the viability of a nonmilitary strategy of crisis intervention. Although the U.N. [United Nations] Security Council had approved the sanctions, the council was never given the opportunity to decide whether or when or how to wage the war conducted in its name. The near-universal condemnation of Iraq's aggression and of support for sanctions was badly eroded by the [US president George H.W.] Bush administration's own aggressive use of "all necessary means." The authorization of "all necessary means" had been promoted, to both the United Nations and Congress, as strengthening Bush's hand to obtain a peaceful settlement—but, whether through intention or impatience, nonmilitary means were never given a fair trial.

The Last Resort Came Too Soon

The just war tradition best serves the imperatives of peacemaking in teaching us that justice is not, first and foremost, a call to arms, to violence and vengeance. In the principle of last resort, the tradition stringently commands peaceful settlement as first resort and as persistent resort. Harold Saunders, former Assistant Secretary of State for Near Eastern Affairs, wrote after the U.S. air assault on Iraq began:

> Learning to work effectively in our changing world requires us not just to give lip service to the old notion that war is a last resort. We have to devote all creative energy to imagining new ways of producing results by political

means, since military action is becoming intolerably costly.

When the first bomb dropped in the war to roll back Iraqi aggression, the hope of using the Gulf crisis of 1990–91 to establish a new world order was seriously undercut.

The practical question is whether and how policymakers can devise ways of confronting lawless and evil acts effectively by using instruments that will not destroy what they are trying to preserve.

For many who are also concerned with the ethics of policy, a political approach offers the possibility of actions not based mainly on firepower but on the power that emerges from political relationships built on mutual consent and shared purposes.

In the biblical story, the understanding of justice arises from the primitive notion of unlimited revenge and moves to proportional retaliation, to the renunciation of vengeance, to the disclaiming of ultimate judgment on the sins of others, to the faithful conviction that *justice is lovingkindness*, for justice is grounded in the love and mercy of God. That affirmation does not settle the old debates between pacifists and just war advocates, but it does command an ethic of justice that is indivisible from peacemaking. In the *shalom* of God and God's good creation, justice and

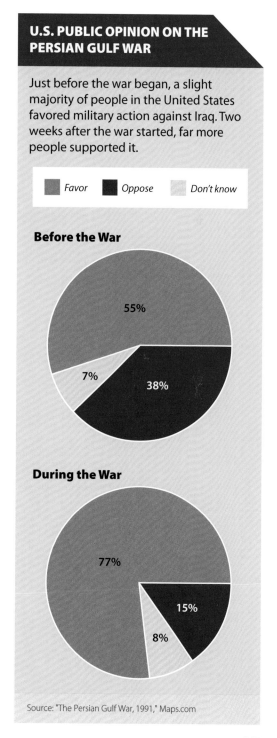

U.S. PUBLIC OPINION ON THE PERSIAN GULF WAR

Just before the war began, a slight majority of people in the United States favored military action against Iraq. Two weeks after the war started, far more people supported it.

Favor · Oppose · Don't know

Before the War

55%

7%

38%

During the War

77%

15%

8%

Source: "The Persian Gulf War, 1991," Maps.com

> Justice and peace do not contradict each other: they are one.

peace do not contradict each other: they are one.

Such an ethic will nerve the creation of transnational institutions of community and common security in which all nations, the most powerful and the least powerful, are alike subject to the sanctions of equity and of law. And it will nurture the ways of both peaceful change and peaceful settlement, because even for the most justifiable of just causes, war has truly become a last, last resort—and will even then most likely be a terrible injustice and an immeasurably tragic blunder.

Israel Played a Vital Role in Helping the US Effort

Mitchell Bard

Through both restraint as well as direct actions, Israel provided vital support to the US-led coalition, says Mitchell Bard in the following viewpoint. He cites sixteen specific examples, including a variety of Israeli-made war equipment and Israeli military data about Iraq. The fact that Israel did not fight Iraq directly was remarkable, the author says, given the severe threats made by Saddam Hussein and his associates, as well as their Scud missile attacks on Israel. Mitchell Bard is executive director of the American-Israeli Cooperative Enterprise and director of the Jewish Virtual Library.

S ince coming to power, Iraqi President Saddam Hussein had been a leader of the rejectionist Arab states and one of the most belligerent foes of Israel. On

---

SOURCE. Mitchell Bard, "The Gulf War," *Jewish Virtual Library*, 2010. Copyright © 2010 by the American-Israeli Cooperative Enterprise. Reproduced by permission of the American-Israeli Cooperative Enterprise.

April 2, 1990, Saddam's rhetoric became more threatening: "I swear to God we will let our fire eat half of Israel if it tries to wage anything against Iraq." Saddam said his nation's chemical weapons capability was matched only by that of the United States and the Soviet Union, and that he would annihilate anyone who threatened Iraq with an atomic bomb by the "double chemical."

> After Saddam used chemical weapons against his own Kurdish population in Halabja in 1988, few people doubted his willingness to use nuclear weapons against Jews in Israel.

Several days later, Saddam said that war with Israel would not end until all Israeli-held territory was restored to Arab hands. He added that Iraq could launch chemical weapons at Israel from several different sites. The Iraqi leader also made the alarming disclosure that his commanders had the freedom to launch attacks against Israel without consulting the high command if Israel attacked Iraq. The head of the Iraqi Air Force subsequently said he had orders to strike Israel if the Jewish State launched a raid against Iraq or any other Arab country.

On June 18, 1990, Saddam told an Islamic Conference meeting in Baghdad: "We will strike at [the Israelis] with all the arms in our possession if they attack Iraq or the Arabs." He declared "Palestine has been stolen," and exhorted the Arab world to "recover the usurped rights in Palestine and free Jerusalem from Zionist captivity."

Iraq's Arms Proliferation

Saddam's threat came in the wake of revelations that Britain and the United States foiled an attempt to smuggle American-made "krytron" nuclear triggers to Iraq. Britain's MI6 intelligence service prepared a secret assessment three years earlier that Hussein had ordered an all-out effort to develop nuclear weapons. After Saddam used chemical weapons against his own Kurdish population in Halabja in 1988, few people doubted his willingness to use nuclear weapons against Jews in Israel if he had the opportunity.

Israeli fears were further raised by reports in the Arabic press, beginning in January 1990, that Jordan and Iraq had formed "joint military battalions" drawn from the various ground, air and naval units. "These battalions will serve as emergency forces to confront any foreign challenge or threat to either of the two countries," one newspaper said. In addition, the two countries were said to have formed a joint air squadron. This was to be the first step toward a unified Arab corps, Jordanian columnist Mu'nis al-Razzaz disclosed. "If we do not hurry up and start forming a unified military Arab force, we will not be able to confront the Zionist ambitions supported by U.S. aid," he said. Given the history of Arab alliances forming as a prelude to planning an attack, Israel found these developments worrisome.

In April 1990, British customs officers found tubes about to be loaded onto an Iraqi-chartered ship that were believed to be part of a giant cannon that would enable Baghdad to lob nuclear or chemical missiles into Israel or Iran. Iraq denied it was building a "supergun," but, after the war, it was learned that Iraq had built such a weapon.

Iraq emerged from its war with Iran with one of the largest and best-equipped military forces in the world. In fact, Iraq had one million battletested troops, more than 700 combat aircraft, 6,000 tanks, ballistic missiles and chemical weapons. Although the U.S. and its allies won a quick victory, the magnitude of Hussein's arsenal only became clear after the war when UN [United Nations] investigators found evidence of a vast program to build chemical and nuclear weapons.

Iraq also served as a base for several terrorist groups that menaced Israel, including the PLO [Palestine Liberation Organization] and Abu Nidal's Fatah Revolutionary Council.

After the Iraqi invasion of Kuwait, Saddam Hussein consistently threatened to strike Israel if his country was attacked. If the U.S. moves against Iraq, he said in December 1990, "then Tel Aviv will receive the next attack, whether or not Israel takes part." At a press conference, following his January 9, 1991, meeting with [US] Secretary of State James Baker, Iraqi Foreign Minister Tariq Aziz was asked if the war starts, would Iraq attack Israel. He replied bluntly: "Yes. Absolutely, yes."

Ultimately, Saddam carried out his threat.

Iraq's Nuclear Development Was Substantial

In 1981, Israel became convinced Iraq was approaching the capability to produce a nuclear weapon. To preempt the building of a weapon that would undoubtedly be directed against them, the Israelis launched their surprise attack, destroying the Osirak nuclear complex. At the time, Israel was widely criticized. On June 19, the UN Security Council unanimously condemned the raid. Critics minimized the importance of Iraq's nuclear program, claiming that because Baghdad had signed the Nuclear Non-Proliferation Treaty and permitted its facilities to be inspected, Israeli fears were baseless.

It was not until after Iraq invaded Kuwait that U.S. officials began to acknowledge publicly that Baghdad was developing nuclear weapons and that it was far closer to reaching its goal than previously thought. Again, many critics argued the Administration was only seeking a justification for a war with Iraq.

Months later, after allied forces had announced the destruction of Iraq's nuclear facilities, UN inspectors found Saddam's program to develop weapons was far more extensive than even the Israelis believed. Analysts had thought Iraq was incapable of enriching uranium for bombs, but Saddam's researchers used several methods (including one thought to be obsolete) that were believed

Photo on previous page: Israel aided the allied forces in a number of noncombat roles, including manufacturing parts of the Tomahawk cruise missile used by the US Navy. (Getty Images.)

> "Israeli concerns proved justified after the war began and Iraq fired 39 Scud missiles at its civilian population centers."

to have made it possible for Iraq to have built at least one bomb.

Prior to [US] President George [H.W.] Bush's announcement of Operation Desert Storm, critics of Israel were claiming the Jewish State and its supporters were pushing Washington [D.C.] to start a war with Iraq to eliminate it as a military threat. President Bush made the U.S. position clear, however, in his speech on August 2, 1990, saying that the United States has "longstanding vital interests" in the Persian Gulf. Moreover, Iraq's "naked aggression" violated the UN charter. The President expressed concern for other small nations in the area as well as American citizens living or working in the region. "I view a fundamental responsibility of my Presidency [as being] to protect American citizens."

Over the course of the Gulf crisis, the President and other top Administration officials made clear the view that U.S. interests—primarily oil supplies—were threatened by the Iraqi invasion of Kuwait. Most Americans agreed with the President's decision to go to war. For example, the *Washington Post*/ABC News Poll on January 16, 1991, found that 76% of Americans approved of the U.S. going to war with Iraq and 22% disapproved.

It is true that Israel viewed Iraq as a serious threat to its security given its leadership of the rejectionist camp. Israeli concerns proved justified after the war began and Iraq fired 39 Scud missiles at its civilian population centers. The Bush Administration had promised to prevent Iraq from attacking Israel, but the U.S. troops assigned to scour the desert for Scud missiles had poor intelligence and failed to destroy a single real missile (they did destroy several decoys) in nearly 2,500 missions.

Israel has never asked American troops to fight its battles. Although Israeli forces were prepared to participate in the Gulf War, they did not because the United

States asked them not to. Even after the provocation of the Scud missile attacks, Israel assented to U.S. appeals not to respond.

How Israel Aided the Allies

Israel was never expected to play a major role in hostilities in the Gulf. American officials knew the Arabs would not allow Israel to help defend them; they also knew U.S. troops would have to intervene because the Gulf states could not protect themselves.

Israel's posture reflected a deliberate political decision in response to American requests. Nevertheless, it did aid the United States' successful campaign to roll back Iraq's aggression. For example:

- The IDF [Israel Defense Forces] was the sole military force in the region that could successfully challenge the Iraqi army. That fact, which Saddam Hussein understood, was a deterrent to further Iraqi aggression.

- By warning that it would take military measures if any Iraqi troops entered Jordan, Israel, in effect, guaranteed its neighbor's territorial integrity against Iraqi aggression.

- The United States benefited from the use of Israeli-made Have Nap air-launched missiles on its B52 bombers. The Navy, meanwhile, used Israeli Pioneer pilotless drones for reconnaissance in the Gulf.

- Israel provided mine plows that were used to clear paths for allied forces through Iraqi minefields.

- Mobile bridges flown directly from Israel to Saudi Arabia were employed by the U.S. Marine Corps.

- Israeli recommendations, based upon system performance observations, led to several software changes that made the Patriot a more capable missile defense system.

- Israel Aircraft Industries developed conformal fuel

tanks that enhanced the range of F15 aircraft. These were used in the Gulf.

- General Dynamics has implemented a variety of Israeli modifications to improve the worldwide F16 aircraft fleet, including structural enhancements, software changes, increased capability landing gear, radio improvements and avionic modifications.

- An Israeli-produced targeting system was used to increase the Cobra helicopter's night-fighting capabilities.

- Israel manufactured the canister for the highly successful Tomahawk missile.

- Night-vision goggles used by U.S. forces were supplied by Israel.

- A low-altitude warning system produced and developed in Israel was utilized on Blackhawk helicopters.

- Other Israeli equipment provided to U.S. forces included flack vests, gas masks and sandbags.

- Israel offered the United States the use of military and hospital facilities. U.S. ships utilized Haifa port shipyard maintenance and support on their way to the Gulf.

- Israel destroyed Iraq's nuclear reactor in 1981. Consequently, U.S. troops did not face a nuclear-armed Iraq.

- Even in its low-profile mode, Israeli cooperation was extremely valuable: Israel's military intelligence had focused on Iraq much more carefully over the years than had the U.S. intelligence community. Thus, the Israelis were able to provide Washington with detailed tactical intelligence on Iraqi military activities. [US] Defense Secretary Richard Cheney said, for example, that the U.S. utilized Israeli information about western Iraq in its search for Scud missile launchers.

The Cost to Israel Was Substantial

Israel benefited from the destruction of Iraq's military capability by the United States-led coalition, but the cost was enormous. Even before hostilities broke out, Israel had to revise its defense budget to maintain its forces at a heightened state of alert. The Iraqi missile attacks justified Israel's prudence in keeping its air force flying round the clock. The war required the defense budget to be increased by more than $500 million. Another $100 million boost was needed for civil defense.

The damage caused by the 39 Iraqi Scud missiles that landed in Tel Aviv and Haifa was extensive. Approximately 3,300 apartments and other buildings were affected in the greater Tel Aviv area. Some 1,150 people who were evacuated had to be housed at a dozen hotels at a cost of $20,000 per night.

> A total of 74 people died as a consequence of Scud attacks. Two died in direct hits, four from suffocation in gas masks and the rest from heart attacks.

Beyond the direct costs of military preparedness and damage to property, the Israeli economy was also hurt by the inability of many Israelis to work under the emergency conditions. The economy functioned at no more than 75 percent of normal capacity during the war, resulting in a net loss to the country of $3.2 billion.

The biggest cost was in human lives. A total of 74 people died as a consequence of Scud attacks. Two died in direct hits, four from suffocation in gas masks and the rest from heart attacks.

A U.N. committee dealing with reparation claims against Iraq dating to the 1991 Gulf War approved more than $31 million to be paid to Israeli businesses and individuals. The 1999 decision stemmed from a 1992 Security Council decision calling on Iraq to compensate victims of the Gulf War. In 2001, the United Nations Compensation Commission awarded $74 million to

Israel for the costs it incurred from Iraqi Scud missile attacks during the Gulf War. The Commission rejected most of the $1 billion that Israel had requested.

The United States Can Preserve a Structure for Mideast Peace

William J. Perry

In the Gulf War, US forces were helped by the Iraqi leadership's misjudgments, but what was crucial to the coalition's overwhelming military victory was a set of advantages that the United States should continue to safeguard and be ready to apply, writes William J. Perry, who later became head of the Defense Department. Beyond superior leadership and troop training, certain high-tech aspects should enable the United States to deter potential conflict in the Middle East and elsewhere—as well as defeat enemies if conflict does break out—Perry maintains. US Secretary of Defense from 1994 to 1997, William J. Perry has been chairman of the firm Technology Strategies and Alliances and a professor and director of international security and strategic studies at Stanford University.

SOURCE. William J. Perry, "Desert Storm and Deterrence," *Foreign Affairs*, vol. 70, no. 4, Fall 1991. Copyright © 1991 by the Council on Foreign Relations, Inc. Reprinted by permission of *Foreign Affairs*. www.ForeignAffairs.com.

In Operation Desert Storm the United States employed for the first time a new class of military systems that gave American forces a revolutionary advance in military capability. Key to this capability is a new generation of military support systems—intelligence sensors, defense suppression systems and precision guidance subsystems—that serve as "force multipliers" by increasing the effectiveness of U.S. weapon systems. An army with such technology has an overwhelming advantage over an army without it, much as an army equipped with tanks would overwhelm an army with horse cavalry.

This new conventional military capability adds a powerful dimension to the ability of the United States to deter war. While it is certainly not as powerful as nuclear weapons, it is a more credible deterrent, particularly in regional conflicts vital to U.S. national interests. It can play a potentially significant role in deterring those regional conflicts that would involve the confrontation of armored forces (as opposed to guerrilla wars). With the increasing proliferation of modern weapons in politically unstable parts of the world, those types of wars might be expected to occur with increasing frequency. The new military capability can also serve as a credible deterrent to a regional power's use of chemical weapons. It should also strengthen the already high level of deterrence of a major war in Europe or Korea. The United States can now be confident that the defeat of a conventional armored assault in those regions could be achieved by conventional military forces, which could enable the United States to limit the role of its nuclear forces to the deterrence of nuclear attack.

That the United States has achieved a revolutionary advance in military capability is suggested by the results of the Gulf War. One overall measure of performance is the relatively low number of coalition losses: tanks destroyed, prisoners captured and, not least, casualties incurred. These losses were so lopsided—roughly

a thousand to one—that there is virtually no historical precedent. It is tempting to conclude, as some have done, that these low figures were attributable simply to the incompetence of the Iraqi military. Indeed the Soviet foreign minister, Aleksandr A. Bessmertnykh, appearing before the Supreme Soviet to discuss the performance of Soviet-supplied air defenses in Iraq, said that the failure was "not a reflection of a weakness of combat equipment. Ultimately equipment is good when it is in good hands." This explanation ignores two important realities: the size and capability of the Iraqi armed forces, and the devastating assault to which they were subjected during the air war.

A US soldier uses an Army computer. The United States' technological superiority over Iraq helped lead to an overwhelming coalition victory. (Time & Life Pictures/Getty Images.)

> *The combination of build-up time and bases available largely offset what otherwise would have been a significant geographical advantage for the Iraqis.*

Prior to the Gulf War, Iraq was reputed to have the fourth-largest army in the world. It was one of the most formidable regional military powers, with over a million men in its army, almost half of whom were in the Kuwaiti theater. Most Iraqi officers had gained recent combat experience in the Iran-Iraq War. Iraqi forces were equipped with large quantities of Soviet equipment, mostly modern, as well as some Western equipment, including Mirage aircraft and Exocet missiles. They had a dense air defense system, a large number of mobile missiles, 4,000 tanks, 3,000 modern long-range artillery and a demonstrated capability to deliver chemical weapons both by air and artillery. Iraq also had a unitary force operating within a few hundred miles of its supply base, while the United States led a disparate coalition some 6,000 miles from its primary supply base.

The Coalition Forces Had Many Advantages

Why, then, were the U.S.-led coalition forces able to defeat the Iraqis so quickly, so decisively and with so few losses?

There were many significant factors favoring the coalition forces, some of which were unique to Desert Storm and cannot be counted on in any future conflict. Foremost among these were the quality and quantity of Saudi air bases and the ready supply of fuel in the theater. Because of Saddam Hussein's political misjudgments the coalition forces had more than five months to deploy and organize. The combination of build-up time and bases available largely offset what otherwise would have been a significant geographical advantage for the Iraqis.

Other factors favoring the coalition will be applicable, however, to a wide variety of military contingencies.

Foremost among these was a great advantage in leadership. The leadership of the coalition was superb, and the diverse military forces operated with an unprecedented unity, which was greatly facilitated by the command authority given to General Colin Powell and General H. Norman Schwarzkopf by the Goldwater-Nichols Defense Reorganization Act. The Iraqi leadership, on the other hand, made serious strategic blunders, most notably allowing the five-month buildup. Even at a distance of 7,000 miles, U.S. air logistical support was outstanding and, after a slow start, the 13,000 mile sealift also became effective. In contrast Iraqi supply lines were essentially cut off early in the air war by the coalition's successful interdiction campaign.

Of course no military operation can be successful with poorly trained troops, and the U.S. military demonstrated that its forces were superbly trained. With an average service time of seven years and training time of two years, the all-volunteer force was notably better trained and motivated than the draftee force that the United States fielded in the Vietnam War. More generally the coalition forces had a significant advantage in training, and motivation over the Iraqi forces, whose combat experience with Iran prepared them for a different type of war, and whose initial doubts about the wisdom and justice of their cause were greatly amplified by the pounding they took during the air war.

But all of these advantages combined do not account for a thousand-to-one discrepancy in performance. A significant part of that edge can be attributed to the revolutionary new military technology used by U.S. forces for the first time in the Gulf War. . . .

Three Key Factors Provide the U.S. Advantage

Countries all over the world will conduct their own analyses of the coalition's military success, and some will try to emulate the technical systems critical to that success. There is no secret about how these systems were developed in the United States. In the 1970s U.S. defense officials saw the opportunity to exploit the new developments in microelectronics and computers to great advantage in military applications. The Defense Department conceived, developed, tested, produced and deployed the systems embodying the new technologies. Finally, the U.S. military developed the tactics for using the new systems, and conducted extensive training with them, mostly under simulated field conditions.

> The United States must control the sale of the systems that are key to the offset strategy: intelligence sensors, Stealth aircraft and precision-guided weapons.

To sustain the U.S. position of leadership in this new military capability, it is neither necessary nor sufficient to control the sale of technology or components. Indeed, even if Washington [D.C.] tried, it could not control this technology. With the exception of Stealth, the underlying technology of these new weapon systems as well as the components imbedded in them can be found in commercial products that have been on the market for five to ten years. The U.S. advantage in this new military technology is not in components, but in systems, training and operational experience.

To sustain this advantage the United States must control the sale of the systems that are key to the offset strategy: intelligence sensors, Stealth aircraft and precision-guided weapons. Even if the United States maintains strict control over the sale of these systems, other nations will gain this capability in time, but not without substantial investment over many years. Just how long the United States maintains its advantage depends on how consistently it constrains the sale of this current generation of weapons, and how effectively it develops the next generation.

While this new military capability will add a new dimension to deterrence, it also has significant limitations. It will not add to the ability of the United States to deter a nuclear attack; for the foreseeable future, that deterrence will depend on the strength of U.S. nuclear forces. Also, the new capability will be quite limited in its effectiveness in any regional conflicts that are basically civil wars or dominated by guerrilla warfare. No one should be deluded into believing that the military capability that can easily defeat an army with 4,000 tanks in a desert is going to be the decisive factor in a jungle or urban guerrilla war.

A central national security issue for the United States in the 1990s will be how to use this remarkable new military capability wisely. This will require a national security policy that constrains the sale of systems critical to the offset strategy so that the United States protects its advantage, manages the declining defense budget with an investment strategy that extends its advantage, guards against the hubris of believing that this new military capability solves all of its national security problems, and positions its foreign policy so that the United States does not become either the world's policeman or the world's bully. Clearly the United States does not want to spend the rest of the decade fighting regional conflicts. The key to avoiding such entanglements is to use its new strength to deter these conflicts rather than fight them.

The Region's Power Structure Changed Considerably

Saul B. Cohen

In this viewpoint written shortly after the Persian Gulf War ended, possibilities are high for Egypt to become the most influential Arab country in the region and for Israel to reach peace agreements with its neighbors. To balance the United States' newly demonstrated dominance, Europe could become a friendly rival for Middle East influence, a competition that would increase regional stability, author Saul B. Cohen suggests. But peace within Iraq itself is far from assured. Professor Saul B. Cohen has been editor of the three-volume *Columbia Gazeteer of the World,* president of the Association of American Geographers, and a member of the New York State Board of Regents.

SOURCE. Saul B. Cohen, "The Geopolitical Aftermath of the Gulf War," *Focus*, vol. 41, issue 2, Summer 1991. Copyright © 1991 by The American Geographical Society. Reproduced by permission of The American Geographical Society.

When the Gulf War was initiated by the allies on January 16, 1991, many heralded it as a "defining" war. The war's aftermath would include a new order for the Persian Gulf and the Middle East as a whole. Forty-four days of battle did lead to a decisive defeat of the Iraqi military dictator who had seized and looted Kuwait. However, the end of the fighting and Iraq's acceptance of the cease-fire did not bring peace.

What followed, instead, was internal uprising, encouraged by America's call for the overthrow of Saddam Hussein. American support went no further, and the rebelling Shia of the south and Kurds of the north were ruthlessly repressed by Iraqi troops who used those tanks, helicopter gunships and fixed-wing aircraft that had escaped destruction during the war.

Then followed the massive flight of 1.75 million Kurds to the mountains near and across the Turkish and Iranian borders. Tens of thousands of Shia also sought refuge in southwestern Iran and in the occupation zone of southern Iraq from which the allied troops have been mostly withdrawn. A twelve-mile-wide demilitarized zone between Iraq and Kuwait was established under United Nations [UN] supervision, but the U.N. has no mandate to protect refugee camps within the zone.

In an effort to protect the fleeing Kurds from continued attack by Iraqi troops and to coax them back from the Turkish frontier, the allies created a 60-mile-deep zone of "safe haven" in the plains and valleys of northern Iraq. Camps have been set up near such Kurdish centers as Zakho, Amaduja and Mosul, in an effort to provide food, clothing and shelter to up to 500,000 to 750,000 Kurds who have fled their cities, towns and villages. Reluctantly and belatedly, the United States responded to Britain and Europe's initial call to establish this region of refuge. Thus, allied troops departed from the south to be replaced by unarmed United Nations forces.

Many Kurds fled Iraq into Turkey and elsewhere after a failed Kurdish uprising against Saddam Hussein. Although Iraq no longer had the resources to fight external enemies, it did fight against Kurds in its own territory. (Getty Images.)

It was politically more complicated for the allies to mount a similar rescue effort for the million Kurds who have fled eastward to Iran, and none was made. Geographically those Kurds could not reach the allied Safe Haven Zone along the Turkish frontier, for they would have to cross territory controlled by the Iraqi army. However, Germany initiated a program with Iran, using German troops to help bring food and supplies to the refugees there. The importance of this initiative was that it not only paved the way for a large-scale Western relief effort, but also portended a broader Western opening to Iran. Some Shia who sought refuge in Iraq's southern marsh area near the Iranian border remain exposed to

Iraqi attack, so that the final story of the revolt in the south has yet to be written.

At Present, Iraq Can Fight Only Itself

Peace has not yet come to the Gulf and the region because the embers of war still smoulder. But if decisive military victory has not yet brought definitive resolution of conflict, it has triggered forces that provide geopolitical direction for the region in the post-war period.

First, Iraq under Saddam Hussein is thoroughly devastated. It can still wage war against its own people, but not against its neighbors. The regime was able to repress the Shia and Kurdish rebellions with the savagery and ruthlessness which has for so long been its hallmark. It was able to do so under the perverted international norm that also sanctioned effective military action to protect Kuwait's national integrity, but did nothing to save individual lives.

> Iraq has lost its capacity to wage war against neighboring states.

The rule of law which restored sovereignty to Kuwait guards against outside interference in the internal affairs of a sovereign state. International tribunals may some day bring Saddam Hussein to justice for human rights violations and crimes against his own people as well as Kuwaitis. However, this is little comfort to those who have been killed or who have died from starvation in the postwar war, or to their families.

On the other hand, Iraq has lost its capacity to wage war against neighboring states, a capacity that it has exercised in the past decade against Iran, Kuwait, Saudi Arabia and Israel. It can no longer bully or blackmail other states. The Iraqi dream of hegemony over the region has come to naught—the nightmare that the new Nebuchadnezzar [an ancient king who conquered Jerusalem] will sweep through the Middle East is over.

Iraq's nuclear and chemical/biological weapons capacities have been uncovered. Until the stock and facilities are dismantled, Iraq can expect to remain isolated from the outside world.

Whether Iraq ultimately rebuilds in its present centralized state form, or as a federation of a relatively autonomous Kurdish north, Sunni Arab center and Shia Arab south, it will have to pursue policies of accommodation not conflict. The United Nations resolutions which were imposed upon it offer no alternative.

The same considerations of regional security and stability that motivated the allies to deprive Iraq of its international war-making capacities are also likely to protect it from dismemberment. Economic rehabilitation and a focus on civilian not military investments lie ahead for Iraq. Moreover, repairing its international relations means acceptance of the boundary that runs down the thalweg, the deepest point in the main navigable channel of the Shattal-Arab. Refusal to accept this boundary was a major cause of the war with Iran. It also means renouncing its claims upon Kuwait for Waraba and Bubiyan islands and the southern tip of the Rumailah oil field.

> The Saudis cannot protect themselves, no matter how many tens of billions of dollars of new weapons they purchase.

Kuwait and Saudi Arabia Are Vulnerable

Kuwait, the victim of Iraq's aggression, will never be the same after what has happened. Environmentally, socially and politically it has experienced an earthquake. Not only is the aftershock likely to bring political reform and a constitutional monarchy, it may well lead to a genuine nation-building effort. The patience of those who remained in Kuwait to resist the Iraqi invasion while the royal family fled is being sorely tried by the slow pace of democratic reforms. Until now the Kuwaitis have never taken full responsibility for operating their own national state. Rather, they have behaved like the penthouse occupants of a building that they own but that was constructed and is operated and largely occupied by others.

Saudi Arabia's military and social vulnerability has also been exposed. The Saudis cannot protect themselves, no matter how many tens of billions of dollars of new weapons they purchase to add to their existing arsenal. If they believe that a permanent American military umbrella is their answer, they will be disappointed. Neither the U.S. Congress nor the American public is likely to support such intervention, and it would provoke serious opposition within much of the Middle East. Moreover, such a presence offers no real guarantee of the Kingdom's present internal order.

A more plausible scenario is for Egypt to emerge as the dominant power and protector of Saudi Arabia. It is now well-positioned to take the lead in fashioning a defense against Iran or a revived Iraq. However, it is unlikely that Egypt would oppose pressures for internal Saudi reform—for women's rights and for free expression. In fact, depending upon the stability of its government or a change in its governance structure, Egypt might emerge as the champion of political change in Saudi Arabia.

Yemen backed the wrong horse in the Gulf War. Its economic situation has deteriorated owing to the expulsion from Saudi Arabia of a million Yemeni workers. In addition, the diminished role of the Soviet Union in the Red Sea and the African Horn has undercut the radical Marxist influences of South Yemen. As a result, Yemen has little alternative but to turn away from the radical Arab camp and the USSR [Union of Soviet Socialist Republics] and towards the victorious Arab states and the West. Egypt especially has regained its regional influence in southwest Arabia. In fact, a southern tier of Middle Eastern states under Egypt's leadership, a structure that has long tempted geopolitical speculation, could be in the offing. . . .

A Chance for Peace with Israel

With the changing status of its surrounding Arab states and the diminished power of the PLO [Palestine Liberation Organization], Israel has an enormous peace opportunity. The opportunity is enhanced by the American, European, Soviet, and United Nations joint commitment to facilitate and guarantee a peace. The present diplomatic joustings over how to start negotiations are important, and yet seem to be a dance of the irrelevant. The heart of the matter is implementation of U.N. Resolutions #242 and #238. These resolutions, passed following the 1967 Six Day War [in which Israel seized Arab land], call for the rights of all peoples to self-determination, for Israel to return all occupied territory, and for all parties to recognize the legality of pre-war international boundaries.

In 1968, the Arabs rejected this formula of "land for peace" and Israel accepted it. Israel then was governed by the Labor party. At that time, the Likud [a major Israeli political party] bolted from a national unity coalition because it would not accept the United Nations mandate. Now the Likud is in power. It and its right-wing allies remain adamantly opposed to #242. Indeed, it tries to sidestep the issue by insisting that the return of the Sinai Peninsula to Egypt has already fulfilled the U.N. resolution.

If the Arabs want land and freedom from Israeli occupation, they have to offer up recognition of Israel, respect for its security and assurances of a "warm" not "cold" peace. Under those circumstances, the current Israeli government, which is forthrightly committed to West Bank annexation, will probably not be able to cling to power, or will have to make a radical volte-face to cling to its ruling position. Israel's historic record in support of Palestine partition, wide-spread public realization that the next war will be a devastating high tech war, even if Israeli military superiority will in all likelihood prevail, and the problems of the economy, especially in view of the massive Soviet immigration, all suggest that Israelis will opt for a reasonable compromise. . . .

Other consequences of the war also warrant attention. There clearly is a need to develop an international prohibition against the use of environmental destruction as a weapon. In addition, the war brought home the vulnerability of desalination plants and oil pipeline transitways, but underscored their value as well. A post-war question to be considered is how have-not nations which possess valuable land transitways and freshwater supplies can gain a larger return on these assets.

Finally, the Gulf War marked a sea-change in the impact upon the region by outside powers. For four decades, the United States and the USSR have been instrumental in making a shatterbelt, a region of continually changing country boundaries and names, of the Middle East. Now, in 1991, there is one dominant force, that of the United States.

> Arms transfers were part of the Cold War balancing process. They have no place in the quest for genuine regional stability.

The presence of only one intrusive power is destabilizing. Imposition of a Pax Americana [American Peace] upon the region is neither desirable nor feasible. Certainly no one longs for a return of the status-quo-ante of the 1950s to 1970s. Then the Middle East was a tinderbox. The superpowers were the fulcrums or balancers. They maintained arms parity between client states, and imposed an end to conflicts when their clients were threatened with destruction, or when they feared that they might have to become directly involved. This cycle of aiding and abetting tension and conflict created a wildly swinging seesaw.

To achieve new regional stability, there is need for a second and balancing intrusive power. In all likelihood, this will be Europe. Should the European Community emerge as an independent force in Middle East affairs, not as a faint echo of U.S. policy, the swings of the regional seesaw will be less rapid, less violent and more predictable. The two major intrusive forces would be friendly competitors, not deadly enemies. Moreover, the Soviet Union, whose influence will be diminished but not disappear, would have more leeway to negotiate its interests between the two other powers.

Arms transfers were part of the Cold War balancing process. They have no place in the quest for genuine regional stability. Resumption of American weapons sales to allied Middle Eastern regional powers or to their subordinate states will only undermine regional stability. It will encourage other outside sellers, as well, and renew the arms race that was so basic to the present unstable situation. Since 1983, approximately 60 percent of the world arms trade has gone to the Middle East. To continue on this path, ostensibly to enhance the defensive capability of friendly Middle Eastern nations, is simply a cynical device to reduce the unit costs of production of high-tech weaponry needed by the Pentagon.

There will continue to be regional change and turbulence in the Middle East. If we have learned our lessons from this catastrophic war, however—a war that brought death to over 100,000 Iraqi soldiers and civilians, and in the post-war upheaval, to countless numbers of Kurds and Shia—it is that we need to adopt geopolitical strategies that treat regional issues holistically. Short-term disequilibrium can never be eliminated, it is part of the process of change. However, change can be managed more prudently and effectively. The challenge that we so successfully faced in the war is even greater in forging the peace. Nations that showed such a capacity for mobilizing for war have the potential to mobilize for peace.

Desert Storm Was a Criminal Assault on Defenseless People

Ramsey Clark

What the US-led coalition did to the people of Iraq was a war crime, contends Ramsey Clark in the following viewpoint. Contrary to myth, more than 90 percent of the US bombing was of the non-precision variety—an assault on defenseless civilians, the viewpoint charges. It says the suffering was made worse after the war ended, as the United States insisted on limiting food and medicine, even for children. The policy was tantamount to genocide, the author concludes. Ramsey Clark served as US attorney general from 1961 to 1968 and later became an internationally known lawyer and human rights activist. After the Persian Gulf War, he initiated the Commission of Inquiry for the International War Crimes Tribunal.

SOURCE. Ramsey Clark, "The Fire This Time," *The Fire This Time: U.S. War Crimes in the Gulf.* Copyright © 1992 by Ramsey Clark. Published by Thunder's Mouth Press. Reproduced by permission of Perseus Book Group.

The assault on Iraq was a war crime containing thousands of individual criminal acts virtually from beginning to end, as any violence against a defenseless adversary must.

[US] President [George H.W.] Bush voiced a different view. On July 1, 1992, the President appeared on CBS's national *This Morning* news, and angrily answered criticism of his policies and conduct toward Iraq. He described those who questioned what happened as "a bunch of people who want to redefine something that was noble and good—Desert Storm—and make it bad."

But look at what was done. Before 1991 was over, more than 250,000 Iraqis and thousands of other nationals were dead as a result of the attack. Most were civilian men, women, children, and infants.

> The bombs killed indiscriminately, hitting Iraqis and others, Muslims and Christians, Kurds and Assyrians, young and old, men and women.

U.S. war casualties, including those who died from U.S. "friendly fire," totaled 148, we are told. Out of an acknowledged 109,876 air sorties, total U.S. aircraft losses were 38, less than the accident rate during war games without live ammunition. The bombs dropped from those aircraft equaled the power of seven Hiroshima bombs. There was no war. There was only a premeditated, calculated slaughter of civilian life and defenseless soldiers.

Television networks turned the 42-day bombardment of Iraq into a running commercial for militarism and U.S. weapons systems. On television, the weapons' accuracy seemed miraculous and the U.S. omnipotent. However, on the ground, the immense air attack against Iraqi cities brought thousands of civilian casualties. Of the 88,500 tons of ordnance rained on Iraq, only 6,520 tons were precision-guided. Nearly 93 percent of the bombing was with dumb bombs, free falling from high altitudes, and no more accurate than the bombs dropped in World War II. The city of Basra was carpet-bombed by B-52s. The bombs killed indiscriminately, hitting Iraqis and others, Muslims and Christians, Kurds and Assyrians, young and old, men and women.

One of the great myths propagated by the Pentagon and the controlled media was that the surgical accuracy of U.S. weapons saved lives. This argument has been used before to justify U.S. violence against its enemies. When U.S. planes bombed the heart of crowded Tripoli in April 1986, Secretary of Defense Caspar Weinberger insisted that it was "impossible" that civilians were killed. In reality, nearly all of the hundreds of casualties were civilians.

An Indiscriminate Assault

What happened in the Gulf was an assault, not a war. There was no combat, no resistance, and few skirmishes. Iraq had no capacity to either attack or defend. It simply endured a pulverizing six-week assault. The U.S. did not lose a single B-52 in combat, as these planes dropped 27,500 tons of bombs. No Iraqi projectile penetrated a single Abrams tank, while the U.S. claimed to destroy 4,300 Iraqi tanks and 1,856 armored vehicles. There were over 1,500 verified kills of Iraqi tanks and armored vehicles by F-111s; the pilots came to call the sport "tank plinking." Finally, tanks and earth-moving equipment buried thousands of Iraqi soldiers—dead, wounded, and alive—while hundreds of tanks, armored vehicles, and artillery pieces and tons of ammunition were seized intact.

Bombs were dropped on civilians and civilian facilities all over Iraq. When I traveled through Iraq on the first anniversary of the bombing to revisit places I had seen during the bombing, I gathered statistics of civilian damage from Iraqi sources. The toll was devastating. Of all the assaults, those on the water and food supply were most deadly and revealing. The attack from the farm to the market was systematic and included every element essential to food production: irrigation, fertilizer, pesticides, tractors. Food importation, which provided 70 percent of the nation's requirements before the war, was vastly reduced by sanctions and other causes. Average daily caloric intake is less than half the prewar level. Malnutrition affects up to half the children in poorer urban areas. With the public debilitated from malnutrition, contaminated water, and disease, and with sanctions causing severe shortages of medical supplies, the Iraqi health care system is unable to care for the sick.

How many did the U.S. kill? General Colin Powell said it was not a figure he was terribly interested in. General William G. Pagonis, stating proudly that this was the first war in modern time where every screwdriver and every nail was accounted for, simultaneously defended General [H. Norman] Schwarzkopf's policy against counting enemy dead. The generals knew but never mentioned that the Geneva Convention of 1949 required them not merely to count enemy dead, but to identify and honor them as well.

The U.S. government and members of the plutocracy are not as unconcerned with the number of Iraqi deaths as they portray. In the summer of 1991 in California's Bohemian Grove, where the rich, the powerful, and the political leadership gather for inspiration and information never shared with the people, former Navy Secretary John Lehman spoke on "smart" weapons. He told a gathering that the Pentagon estimated 200,000 Iraqis killed by the United States during the Gulf War. The public has never officially been told this—and would never have known at all if a *People* magazine journalist had not sneaked on to the Bohemian Grove compound.

Victims Are Dishonored

Somehow, the number of Iraqi deaths has been a minuscule part of the debate over President Bush's handling

Photo on following page: An Iraqi woman walks along the outskirts of Baghdad as the city burns in the background. (Getty Images.)

of the Gulf War, perhaps because the slaughter of dark-skinned people by U.S. weaponry has become all too commonplace. On February 18, Brigadier General Richard Neal, while briefing reporters in Riyadh, observed that the United States wanted to be certain of speedy victory once they committed ground troops to "Indian Country." In two words, he revealed that the U.S. military honors its racist history and intended another slaughter of "savages."

Estimating the numbers of people killed by the U.S. assault is difficult and painful, yet critically important. Each life counts. To understate the casualties by counting only corpses actually found is to conceal the crime, diminish the lessons of history, and hide the truth. To overestimate casualties cheapens the horror of what actually happened by making the truth seem inadequate. Yet an accurate count is impossible under the circumstances, because powerful interests want to control this principal measure of the meaning of war.

Commission research, hearings, documentation, and analyses indicate between 125,000 and 150,000 Iraqi soldiers were killed. There is tragically an all-too-solid basis for believing the early reports of 100,000 military casualties, and in the European press, 200,000 killed. Did not the Pentagon state it would destroy the Iraqi military months before the assault? What could be expected from all that uncontested bombing?

As for civilians, organizations like Greenpeace and MEW, that were unable to send teams into Iraq during the bombing, have estimated less than 3,000 civilian deaths from bombing. The U.S. Census Bureau estimated 5,000 direct civilians deaths from the bombing, and tried to fire its researcher, Beth DaPonte, whose report set the figure at 13,000. But even the 13,000 figure requires a belief in the miraculous when the nationwide assault on civilian life is analyzed. How do you bomb and strafe throughout an entire country, make tens of thousands of sorties with missiles containing every kind of cluster bomb and antipersonnel weapon, destroy 8,400 homes, hundreds of vehicles on highways, thousands of shops, offices, stores, cafes, hotels, plants, bridges, train stations, bus depots, markets, schools, mosques, and bomb shelters, and not kill tens of thousands?

Inestimable Civilian Tragedies

> "How the Iraqis were killed was particularly cruel. Many thousands of civilians died from polluted water."

Experience, reason, and actual counts completed make the 150,000 minimum civilian deaths in Iraq since the beginning of the war until early 1992 a very conservative number. Although the American media saturated the U.S. with reports of Scud missile attacks on Israel, it showed little of the destruction in Iraq. Two Israelis died from two score Scud attacks. This was tragic. A quarter of a million Iraqis, military and civilian, died from 110,000 air attacks. This was genocidal.

How the Iraqis were killed was particularly cruel. Many thousands of civilians died from polluted water. Dehydrated from nausea and diarrhea, craving liquids, they had nothing to drink but more of the water that made them sick. Infants by the tens of thousands died from lack of milk formula and medication. The chronically ill, the sick, and the injured died from lack of medical care, medicine, clean water, and sanitation. Children, the weak, and the elderly died from diseases and malnutrition at several times the normal rate.

Soldiers died when bombs from planes they never saw rained down on them. Communications, supplies, water, food, and command were cut off. They risked death if they tried to move out. Deaths among the wounded ran very high because no evacuation was possible and little medical assistance was available. Thousands of wounded,

The End in Kuwait

One of the controversies concerning how the US side fought involves two roads in Kuwait that became known as the highways of death. On these roads, which run to the border with Iraq, tens of thousands of Iraqi soldiers died in the last days of the war.

Critics charge that the soldiers were retreating—pulling out of Kuwait as demanded by the allied coalition—and there was no need to slaughter them. Journalist Joyce Chediac wrote:

> U.S. planes trapped the long convoys by disabling vehicles in the front, and at the rear, and then pounded the resulting traffic jams for hours. "It was like shooting fish in a barrel," said one U.S. pilot. . . . This one-sided carnage, this racist mass murder of Arab people, occurred while White House spokesman Marlin Fitzwater promised that the U.S. and its coalition partners would not attack Iraqi forces leaving Kuwait.

sick, disoriented, and dead were buried when American tanks and earth-moving equipment bulldozed sand over their trenches. Thousands died from illegal fragmentation bombs, fuel-air explosives, and incineration along stretches of road with names like the seven-mile "Highway of Death." An even more horrific example was the destruction of a nameless 60-mile convoy reported 10 days after the ceasefire. Thousands of Iraqi soldiers died in assaults after the ceasefire. There was a continuing murderous intent to destroy units missed in the general slaughter.

An immediate result of the destruction of targets selected for aerial bombardment was the endangerment of the entire civilian population. Within days after the bombing began on January 17, there was no running water in any city, town, or village in Iraq. There was no electric power, and no communications. There was no air or rail transportation, and very limited bus, taxi, and private car transportation. The whole country was in constant jeopardy of a chance assault from the air.

Fighting Stops, But Children Suffer

The embargo imposed on Iraq since the war by the Sanctions Committee of the UN [United Nations] Security Council, at the insistence of the United States, is further evidence of the intention to destroy civilian life in Iraq. While the United States claims the embargo does not seriously affect the importation of food and medicine, the evidence to the contrary is indisputable. The sanctions constitute a continuing violation of humanitarian law.

By April 1991, doctors were finding among infants many cases of kwashiorkor, an extreme state of malnutrition in which the belly bloats and the arms, legs, and body wither. It had been virtually unknown to Iraqi doctors. By June, *Time* magazine reported that Qadisiyeh Hospital in Baghdad was admitting 10 new cases a day of infants suffering from marasmus, which it described as "an advanced case of malnutrition that causes a child's face and body to become as shriveled and haggard as those of a wizened old man." In October, the most extensive western medical survey of health conditions in Iraq, conducted by Harvard's International Study Team, found child mortality to be three times the prewar level. In February 1992, the director of Qadisiyeh Hospital showed me wards only 25 percent utilized because of the lack of medicine and equipment. He said that, even at this occupancy rate, there were 250 more deaths per month in the hospital than in 1990. Sadly, however, most deaths among the 800,000 population in the slums of Saddam City, which the hospital serves, went unreported.

Infant mortality doubled and in some areas tripled. About 750,000 infants were born in Iraq each year prior to the war. The infant mortality rate in 1989 was 69 per thousand live births. Doubling that rate for an entire year means an additional 51,750 infants would die as a direct result of U.S. bombing and sanctions. Mortality rates among children under five also rose drastically, threatening the majority and taking tens of thousands of young lives. Twenty-nine percent of all children were estimated to suffer severe malnutrition in the winter of 1991–1992. In the neighborhood of Qadisiyeh Hospital, the rate was a horrifying 50 percent. A large percentage of the survivors—a "stunted generation," according to one medical report—will live shorter lives with physical handicaps from malnutrition and disease caused by the destruction of water, sewage, health care, and medical facilities and the shortage of food and medical supplies caused by the embargo.

> A whole nation is being held hostage, tortured with threats, hunger, sickness, and violence.

In late fall 1991, UNICEF [United Nations Children's Fund] predicted 170,000 Iraqi children under six years of age would suffer malnutrition by the end of the year unless drastic relief was provided, and that over half would die. OXFAM [an international confederation of organizations fighting famine and poverty] in late 1991 reported millions of Iraqis were suffering because of the strategic bombing of water, sewage, and health systems. In the face of these facts, the UN Sanctions Committee acceded to U.S. insistence and maintained an embargo which limited food and medicine. A whole nation is being held hostage, tortured with threats, hunger, sickness, and violence, while scores of people die daily. The policy is genocidal and known to be so by the U.S. government and media, the informed public everywhere, the UN membership, and the Sanctions Committee.

President Bush repeatedly urged that aggression must not be rewarded. No one who wants peace will dispute that principle. But when it is remembered that the American assault on Panama eight months earlier was at least as lawless and considerably deadlier, his motives in Iraq must be reexamined. How does the United States explain [invasions, attacks, and scandals in] Grenada, Libya, the Contras, and Panama? And what of the reward the Bush administration sought from the aggression against Iraq?

This is not to suggest that one case of aggression justifies another. It is to show the hypocrisy of the United States' argument and the political motives behind it. The United States wanted to crush Iraq, and it has. It wanted to dominate the region and its resources, and it does. The question now is whether this aggression will be rewarded, or whether the appropriate people will be held accountable.

Arab Leaders Could Have Prevented the War

Majid Khadduri and Edmund Ghareeb

The leaders of Saudi Arabia, Egypt, and Jordan—three of the most prominent Arab nations—proposed negotiations before the war, but didn't push strongly for an agreement, Majid Khadduri and Edmund Ghareeb report in the following viewpoint. Then, when other Arab efforts to persuade Iraq to withdraw from Kuwait were under way, the United States intervened with partisan pressure, the viewpoint contends. It says there was a path for Iraq to pull back with honor and good results, but instead the war happened. Professor Majid Khadduri, author of *The Gulf War,* founded the Center for Middle East Studies at the Johns Hopkins University School of Advanced International Studies. Edmund Ghareeb, a specialist on media affairs, has been an adjunct professor of history at George Washington University.

SOURCE. Majid Khadduri and Edmund Ghareeb, "Conclusion: Was the War Inevitable?" *War in the Gulf 1990–91: The Iraq-Kuwait Conflict and Its Implications.* Copyright © 1997 by Oxford University Press, Inc. Reproduced by permission of Oxford University Press, Inc.

In the case of the Gulf crisis, the Islamic countries were divided into two camps. Countries that supported Iraq were motivated largely by Islamic standards on the grounds that Iraq was the subject of Western (Christian) intervention in Arab (Islamic) lands and, therefore, was bound to defend itself by the *jihad* against the unbelievers as a matter of duty. The countries which sided with Kuwait argued that since Iraq, an Islamic country, attacked another Islamic country, the declaration of *jihad* against unbelievers was irrelevant. Moreover, as Iraq was governed by the Ba'th Party, considered by opponents a secular political party, its declaration of the *jihad* was questioned, although the Ba'th Party has never officially declared the separation of religion from the state.

From the perspective of the advocates of realism and the conspiracy theory, the United States and Britain have consciously used the United Nations [UN] Resolutions presumably for the maintenance of international peace and security—certainly not for justice and human rights as stated in the U.N. Charter (Article 1)—but in reality in pursuit of their vital interests (if not the political ambition of their leaders) which Saddam Husayn [alternate spelling of Hussein] had threatened by his invasion of Kuwait. Kuwait was not the central issue—"the occupation of Kuwait isn't, in itself, a threat to American interests" said one of [US president George H.W.] Bush's advisers—the central issue was the threat to Western, national, vital self interests. Just as Saddam Husayn, according to the conspiracy theory, had invaded Kuwait in order to possess its oil resources and acquire an access to the sea which would enhance his leadership, so were Bush and [British Prime Minister Margaret] Thatcher determined to ensure the availability of oil and enhance their won leadership by preventing him from controlling or blocking free passage of oil through the Gulf.

The purpose of the foregoing theories was essentially to determine the aims and drives of the leaders involved

Egyptian president Husni Mubarak (left) and Saudi Arabia's King Fahd (right) were two of the three Arab leaders who could have stopped the war with proper interventions during the Jidda meetings in July 1990. (Time & Life Pictures/Getty Images.)

in the Gulf crisis, but not to conceptualize achieving peace and justice in the world. True, there were always a few noble voices calling for peace and justice whether through the United Nations or the instrumentality of law and diplomacy. But neither the advocates of realism nor of the conspiracy theory addressed themselves to the question of peace based on justice, as these two ideals are inseparable. There were on more than one occasion possibilities to achieve peace with justice, but none of those who sought to achieve them had succeeded. Why, one may well ask?

A Great Chance Missed

The first and perhaps the most important opportunity to resolve the Gulf crisis was at the Jidda [Saudi Arabia] meeting, held under the auspices of the Saudi government on July 31, 1990. . . . However, neither the Iraqi nor the Kuwaiti delegation was ready to be flexible enough to reach an agreement, as each delegation had been given strict instructions about the fundamental demands that they had been ordered to make firmly. The head of the Kuwaiti delegation, Shaykh Sa'd, claimed that he offered several flexible proposals that might be discussed at the Baghdad meeting, but those proposals seemed to the head of the Iraqi delegation insignificant to warrant holding another meeting in Baghdad, and he left for home when the Iraq Army was ready to march on Kuwait a few hours later.

Had the three Arab leaders—King Fahd of Saudi Arabia, President Husni Mubarak of Egypt, and King Husayn of Jordan—who proposed holding the Jidda meetings in the first place, offered mediation before the Jidda meeting broke down or held an Arab mini-summit and appealed to Iraq and Kuwait to resume negotiations before the crisis had developed, the Western powers could have found no reason to intervene. This was the first and perhaps the most important missed opportunity for an Arab peaceful settlement.

The second opportunity was the personal good offices of two Arab leaders—King Husayn and President Husni Mubarak—who sought, immediately after Iraq's invasion of Kuwait, to persuade Saddam Husayn to withdraw provided negotiations for settlement of the dispute would immediately start. This attempt was important, as it would have met Saddam Husayn's request that any withdrawal would not be preceded by condemnation.

Considering Iraq's invasion of Kuwait a threat to Western vital interests, some members of the Security Council, it will be recalled, moved quickly to adopt the first mandatory resolution demanding the "immediate and unconditional" withdrawal of Iraqi forces on the same day when the invasion of Kuwait started. Four days later, the Security Council adopted another mandatory resolution imposing economic sanctions, which signalled that the Gulf crisis had no longer remained a regional issue. When King Husayn and President Mubarak met at Alexandria to discuss ways and means for an Arab solution, they requested President Bush in a telephone conversation to give them enough time to resolve the crisis. Had Bush allowed the two Arab leaders to carry out their proposed plan, the question of the maintenance of international peace and security might not have arisen nor might not the protection of Western interests have needed foreign intervention. Bush, however, insisted that the invasion was a threat to Western interests and even hesitated to give King Husayn and Mubarak forty-eight hours to do their job. He went as far as to disrupt the cooperative efforts of the Arab leaders by persuading Mubarak to issue a condemnation of the invasion and consequently he sided with him, leaving King Husayn to deal with the crisis alone.

> Western leaders had taken advantage of this situation without giving the Arabs an opportunity to do their job.

Responsibility for this situation might perhaps be equally divided between Western and Arab leaders. As differences among Arab leaders could take quite a while to iron out, Western leaders had taken advantage of this situation without giving the Arabs an opportunity to do their job. When the Arab League finally met in full session to deal with the crisis on August 9–10, 1990, Western intervention had already encouraged several Arab leaders sympathetic with Kuwait to insist on Iraq's withdrawal "immediately and unconditionally," although several other Arab leaders held that a face-saving promise would have encouraged Iraq to withdraw. Moreover, the increasing number of the Security Council Resolutions was overwhelming, which rendered the chances of Arab mediation to achieve peaceful settlement to become almost nil. Several other attempts were made by Western as well as Arab leaders to persuade both Bush to recognize some of Iraq's legitimate security requirements, and Saddam Husayn to withdraw from Kuwait. Neither side was ready to compromise.

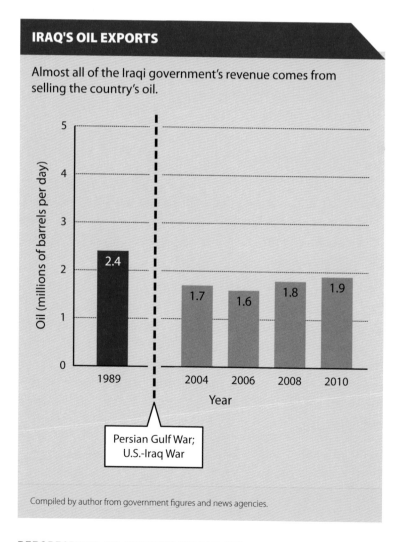

IRAQ'S OIL EXPORTS

Almost all of the Iraqi government's revenue comes from selling the country's oil.

Persian Gulf War; U.S.-Iraq War

Compiled by author from government figures and news agencies.

Leaving Kuwait Could Have Been to Iraq's Gain

Had Saddam Husayn agreed to withdraw from Kuwait, as he was advised by King Husayn, he would have achieved significant advantages to his country and to the Arab world. More specifically, in the words of King Husayn:

1) He would have shown that Iraq's occupation of Kuwait was an "act of self-defence against an inflexible position and not just expansionism";

2) Iraq's achievement in the development of the infrastructure and industrialization of the country would have been preserved;

3) Attention would have been drawn to address the problem of the growing gap between the rich and the poor Arab countries;

4) Attention would have been called to the need to resolve the Palestine problem as a sequel to Iraq's withdrawal from Kuwait; and

5) The United Nations position in the world would have been enhanced by the resolution of the crisis by peaceful means.

The Gulf War was thus not inevitable. Had Western powers been patient in dealing with Arab leaders, or had the Arab leaders acted more quickly before the wheels of Western intervention rolled, the crisis might have been resolved by peaceful means. The lesson to be drawn from this study is that all those who were involved in the crisis on all sides have indeed paid a high price in varying degrees. Nor is it certain that settlement by the use of force can guarantee peace irrespective of justice.

The War Sickened More Than One Fourth of US Troops

Research Advisory Committee on Gulf War Veterans' Illnesses

The most comprehensive scientific study of what became known as Gulf War Syndrome found that about 175,000 US veterans of the war became ill. The following report concludes that the causes of their illnesses were unlike those of any previous wars. One main cause was pills that US commanders handed out to their troops to prevent the possible effects of a nerve gas attack by the enemy. The other main cause was pesticides from various sources. The Research Advisory Committee on Gulf War Veterans' Illnesses was created by Congress to recommend research related to the war.

SOURCE. Research Advisory Committee on Gulf War Veterans' Illnesses, "Gulf War Illness and the Health of Gulf War Veterans: Scientific Findings and Recommendations," November 2008.

Gulf War illness, the multisymptom condition resulting from service in the 1990–1991 Gulf War, is the most prominent health issue affecting Gulf War veterans, but not the only one. The Congressionally-mandated Research Advisory Committee on Gulf War Veterans' Illnesses has reviewed the extensive evidence now available, including important findings from scientific research and government investigations not considered by earlier panels, to determine what is known about the health consequences of military service in the Gulf War. This evidence identifies the foremost causes of Gulf War illness, describes biological characteristics of this condition, and provides direction for future research urgently needed to improve the health of Gulf War veterans.

Gulf War illness is a serious condition that affects at least one fourth of the 697,000 U.S. veterans who served in the 1990–1991 Gulf War. This complex of multiple concurrent symptoms typically includes persistent memory and concentration problems, chronic headaches, widespread pain, gastrointestinal problems, and other chronic abnormalities not explained by well-established diagnoses. No effective treatments have been identified for Gulf War illness and studies indicate that few veterans have recovered over time.

Gulf War illness fundamentally differs from trauma and stress-related syndromes described after other wars. Studies consistently indicate that Gulf War illness is not the result of combat or other stressors and that Gulf War veterans have lower rates of post traumatic stress disorder than veterans of other wars. No similar widespread, unexplained symptomatic illness has been identified in veterans who have served in war zones since the Gulf War, including current Middle East deployments.

Evidence strongly and consistently indicates that two Gulf War neurotoxic exposures are causally associated with Gulf War illness: 1) use of pyridostigmine bromide

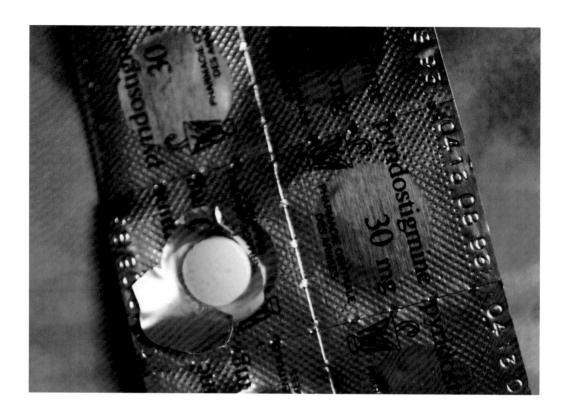

(PB) pills, given to protect troops from effects of nerve agents, and 2) pesticide use during deployment. Evidence includes the consistent association of Gulf War illness with PB and pesticides across studies of Gulf War veterans, identified dose-response effects, and research findings in other populations and in animal models.

For several Gulf War exposures, an association with Gulf War illness cannot be ruled out. These include low-level exposure to nerve agents, close proximity to oil well fires, receipt of multiple vaccines, and effects of combinations of Gulf War exposures. There is some evidence supporting a possible association between these exposures and Gulf War illness, but that evidence is inconsistent or limited in important ways.

Other wartime exposures are not likely to have caused Gulf War illness for the majority of ill veterans. For re-

Pyridostigmine bromide pills—taken by Gulf War soldiers to protect them from nerve agents—have been identified as one of the two most probable causes of Gulf War illness. (Orban Thierry/ Corbis Sygma.)

maining exposures, there is little evidence supporting an association with Gulf War illness or a major role is unlikely based on what is known about exposure patterns during the Gulf War and more recent deployments. These include depleted uranium, anthrax vaccine, fuels, solvents, sand and particulates, infectious diseases, and chemical agent resistant coating (CARC).

Gulf War illness is associated with diverse biological alterations that most prominently affect the brain and nervous system. Research findings in veterans with Gulf War illness include significant differences in brain structure and function, autonomic nervous system function, neuroendocrine and immune measures, and measures associated with vulnerability to neurotoxic chemicals. There is little evidence of peripheral neuropathies in Gulf War veterans.

> "Substantial federal Gulf War research funding has been used for studies that have little or no relevance to the health of Gulf War veterans."

Gulf War illness has both similarities and differences with multisymptom conditions in the general population. Symptom-defined conditions like chronic fatigue syndrome, fibromyalgia, and multiple chemical sensitivity occur at elevated rates in Gulf War veterans, but account for only a small proportion of veterans with Gulf War illness.

Studies indicate that Gulf War veterans have significantly higher rates of amyotrophic lateral sclerosis (ALS) than other veterans, and that Gulf War veterans potentially exposed to nerve agents have died from brain cancer at elevated rates. Although these conditions have affected relatively few veterans, they are cause for concern and require continued monitoring.

Important questions remain about other Gulf War health issues. These include questions about rates of other neurological diseases, cancers, and diagnosed conditions in Gulf War veterans, current information on overall and disease-specific mortality rates in Gulf War veterans, and unanswered questions concerning the health of veterans' children.

Federal Gulf War research programs have not been effective, historically, in addressing priority issues related to Gulf War illness and the health of Gulf War veterans. Substantial federal Gulf War research funding has been used for studies that have little or no relevance to the health of Gulf War veterans, and for research on stress and psychiatric illness. Recent Congressional actions have brought about promising new program developments at the Departments of Defense and Veterans Affairs, but overall federal funding for Gulf War research has declined dramatically since 2001.

A renewed federal research commitment is needed to identify effective treatments for Gulf War illness and address other priority Gulf War health issues. Adequate funding is required to achieve the critical objectives of improving the health of Gulf War veterans and preventing similar problems in future deployments. This is a national obligation, made especially urgent by the many years that Gulf War veterans have waited for answers and assistance. . . .

Evidence Points to Two Main Causes

Seventeen years after the Gulf War, answers to the question of what caused Gulf War illness remain vitally important. An extensive amount of available information now permits an evidence-based assessment of the relationship of Gulf War illness to the many experiences and exposures encountered by military personnel during the Gulf War. The strongest and most consistent evidence from Gulf War epidemiologic studies indicates that use of pyridostigmine bromide (PB) pills and pesticides are significant risk factors for Gulf War illness. The consistency of epidemiologic evidence linking these exposures to Gulf War illness, identified dose-response effects, findings from Gulf War clinical studies, additional research supporting biological plausibility, and the compatibility of these findings with known patterns of exposure during deployment, combine to provide a persuasive case that use of PB pills and pesticides during the 1990–1991 Gulf War are causally associated with Gulf War illness. Gulf War studies also consistently indicate that psychological stressors during deployment are *not* significantly associated with Gulf War illness.

Evidence related to other deployment-related exposures is not as abundant or consistent as evidence related to PB, pesticides, and psychological stressors. For several wartime exposures, there is some evidence supporting a possible association with Gulf War illness, but that evidence is inconsistent or limited in important ways. Clinical studies of Gulf War veterans, studies of other populations exposed to [the chemical weapon] sarin, and findings from animal studies all suggest that low-level nerve agent exposure can produce persistent neurological effects that may be compatible with symptoms of Gulf War illness. Therefore, an association between Gulf War illness and low-level nerve agents cannot be ruled out for those veterans who were exposed. However, inconsistencies in epidemiologic studies and unreliable exposure information preclude a clear evaluation of the extent to which such exposures occurred and may have contributed to Gulf War illness. Limited evidence from several sources also suggests that an association with Gulf War illness cannot be ruled out in relation to combined effects of neurotoxicant exposures, receipt of multiple vaccines, and exposure to the Kuwaiti oil fires, particularly for personnel in close proximity to the burning wells for an extended period.

There is little reliable information from Gulf War studies concerning an association of DU [depleted uranium] or anthrax vaccine to Gulf War illness. The prominence of both exposures in more recent deployments, in

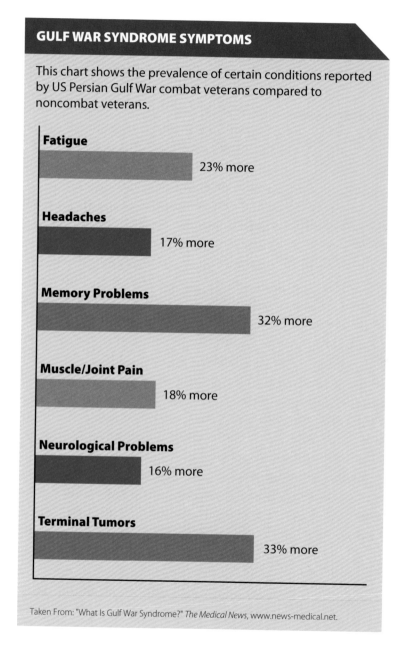

GULF WAR SYNDROME SYMPTOMS

This chart shows the prevalence of certain conditions reported by US Persian Gulf War combat veterans compared to noncombat veterans.

Fatigue

23% more

Headaches

17% more

Memory Problems

32% more

Muscle/Joint Pain

18% more

Neurological Problems

16% more

Terminal Tumors

33% more

Taken From: "What Is Gulf War Syndrome?" *The Medical News*, www.news-medical.net.

the absence of widespread unexplained illness, suggests these exposures are unlikely to have been major causes of Gulf War illness for the majority of affected veterans. Fine blowing sand, solvents, and fuel exposures were also widely encountered in both the 1990–1991 Gulf War and in the current Iraq War and results from studies of Gulf War veterans have not supported an association between these exposures and Gulf War illness. All of the exposures described can be hazardous in some circumstances, however, and some veterans may have experienced adverse effects on a more limited basis. . . .

> The extensive body of scientific research now available consistently indicates that Gulf War illness is real . . . and that few veterans have recovered or substantially improved with time.

Veterans of the 1990–1991 Gulf War had the distinction of serving their country in a military operation that was a tremendous success, achieved in short order. But many had the misfortune of developing lasting health consequences that were poorly understood and, for too long, denied or trivialized. The extensive body of scientific research now available consistently indicates that Gulf War illness is real, that it is the result of neurotoxic exposures during Gulf War deployment, and that few veterans have recovered or substantially improved with time. Addressing the serious and persistent health problems affecting 175,000 Gulf War veterans remains the obligation of the federal government and all who are indebted to the military men and women who risked their lives in Iraq, Kuwait, and Saudi Arabia 17 years ago. This obligation is made more urgent by the length of time Gulf War veterans have waited for answers and assistance.

The Bush Administration Kept the Public from Learning the Whole Truth

Jacqueline Sharkley

What Americans saw, heard, and read about the Persian Gulf War was not the complete story, Jacqueline Sharkley contends in the following viewpoint, because of manipulation by President George H.W. Bush's administration. According to this viewpoint, press restrictions and factual misrepresentations were imposed often not to protect military security, but instead for political reasons. For example, an administration agenda to build support for controversial weapons led to misleading accounts of those weapons' success rates. Jacqueline Sharkley, a University of Arizona journalism professor, writes about free-press issues.

SOURCE. Jacqueline Sharkley, "Desert Storm Disinformation," *The Public i*, Center for Public Integrity, October 1, 2001, www.alternet. org/story/11606/. Copyright © 1991 by the Center for Public Integrity. Reprinted by permission on their website.

A note from The Public i:

   With the United States on the brink of a new war, this time against terrorism, it is useful to recall the restrictions on the news media imposed during the last occasions the United States was on war footing.

   After the U.S. adventures in the Persian Gulf, Grenada and Panama in the 1980s and 1990s, the Center for Public Integrity examined the consequences of those government impositions in a 1991 report, "Under Fire: U.S. Military Restrictions on the Media from Grenada to the Persian Gulf."

   In this edited summary, the report concludes that information about Defense Department activities . . . [was] restricted or manipulated not for national security purposes, but for political purposes—to protect the image and priorities of the Defense Department and its civilian leaders, including the president.

   The recent war in the Persian Gulf has been perceived as a major triumph for U.S. military forces and foreign policy. Victory parades have made front-page news, Gen. H. Norman Schwarzkopf has become a new national hero, and President George Bush has received some of the highest public opinion ratings in history. But one aspect of the conflict has received less attention.

   The Gulf War included unprecedented restrictions on the press by the military, and an extensive campaign by the White House and the Pentagon to influence public opinion by presenting Americans with carefully controlled images and information concerning the conflict and the issues surrounding the Bush administration's decision to use U.S. troops to resolve the crisis. The result was a defeat for the First Amendment guarantee of press freedom and the public's right to independent information about the political decisions that can lead to U.S. military involvement abroad, and the ramifications of such involvement. This study examines the controversies surrounding restrictions on the media during the Gulf

Photo on following page: The Bush administration kept important information from the press during the Gulf War, including facts about the accuracy of the bombs and the extent of civilian casualties. (Time & Life Pictures/Getty Images.)

War and two major U.S. offensive military operations in the 1980s: the invasions of Grenada and Panama.

"Disturbing Pattern of Escalating Control"

Extensive research about military restrictions on the press and the political factors that have contributed to these restrictions during the past 10 years reveals a disturbing pattern of escalating control over media access to information on and off the battlefield. The evidence shows that, increasingly, information about Defense Department activities is being restricted or manipulated not for national security purposes, but for political purposes—to protect the image and priorities of the Defense Department and its civilian leaders, including the president, who is the commander-in-chief of the armed forces.

This pattern is not simply a clash of mentalities between the military and the media. Many crucial decisions about information policies have been made by civilian leaders in the Pentagon and the White House over the objections of military officers who have fought hard to maintain journalists' access to the field and armed forces personnel, and have worked around the clock during operations to assist reporters' and photographers' efforts to present independent information to the American people.

The techniques used by the government to limit and shape news coverage—which have included prohibiting access to military operations and releasing misleading data about U.S. successes and casualties—bring up issues that go far beyond the obvious need to balance military secrecy requirements with the public's right to know. This information-control program has distorted accounts of what occurred during the military operations in Grenada, Panama and the Persian Gulf, has led to false perceptions about the operations' short- and long-term impact on these regions and on U.S. policy, and has threatened the historical record.

Gulf War Aim: "To promote public support for predetermined agendas"

In the months following Operation Desert Storm, considerable evidence has emerged that the news-management strategy used by the Bush administration was designed not to enable the American people to make an objective evaluation of the events leading up to the conflict and the conduct of the war itself, but to promote public support for predetermined agendas, such as access to oil and support for controversial weapons systems.

Highlights of this evidence include:

Congressional testimony by a former Pentagon official that the Defense Department "doctored" statistics about the success rates of weapons systems in the Gulf to increase public support for the war and congressional support for additional weapons funding.

Congressional testimony by a former Pentagon adviser that the Patriot missiles were not as effective as the Defense Department claimed, and that they may have caused more damage than they prevented.

> The Patriot missiles were not as effective as the Defense Department claimed, and . . . may have caused more damage than they prevented.

Statements by Air Force Chief of Staff Gen. Merrill A. McPeak which indicate that Pentagon videos depicting laser-guided bombs hitting their targets with surgical precision—which were shown repeatedly on the [broadcast] networks and Cable News Network—presented a distorted view of the air war. At a postwar briefing, McPeak released statistics showing that such bombs represented 8.8 percent of the ordnance dropped by U.S. forces on Iraq. The remaining 91.2 percent of the 84,200 tons of bombs dropped by the United States during the conflict were "dumb" bombs that had no precision guidance systems.

Statements indicating that Pentagon briefer Lt. Gen. Thomas Kelly's claims during the first week of the war that bombing missions had an 80 percent success rate were misleading. After repeated questioning by reporters, Defense Department officials clarified that "success" meant a plane had taken off, released its ordnance in the area of the target, and returned to its base. Gen. McPeak admitted during his postwar briefing that during the first 10 days of the air war, the weather was so bad that coalition pilots could not even see 40 percent of their primary targets. Lt. Gen. Kelly later said the problem resulted from a "policy change" about how the term "success rate" should be defined.

> Coalition bombing destroyed health and sanitation facilities, and agricultural production.

Evidence that private video firms interested in producing Gulf War programs that would present the U.S. military effort in a positive light were allowed greater access to the field than journalists. Quantum Diversified, a Minneapolis firm that wanted to make a video featuring the National Guard, spent eight days photographing selected units in the Gulf in October 1990. At the time, reporters sometimes waited weeks to spend brief periods with specific military units. The itinerary for Quantum Diversified—which received technical assistance for the video from NFL Films—was set up with the consent of U.S. Central Command and the help of Pentagon officials, including the Office of the Assistant Secretary of Defense for Public Affairs. When Quantum Diversified wanted to shoot additional footage in March, Pentagon officials again arranged space on a military flight, and Central Command sent a message to Army, Air Force, Marine and Navy officials stating the crew had theater clearance. Maj. Robert Dunlap of the National Guard

Bureau's Public Affairs Office in the Pentagon said the Defense Department was happy to help because Quantum Diversified wasn't a "fly-by-night" operation that would "put out a bunch of bad news stories."

Indications that the Pentagon was unwilling to disclose what it knew about the likelihood of civilian casualties caused by U.S. and Allied bombing. During Pentagon briefings, officials repeatedly stressed that U.S. planes were avoiding civilian targets, but little was said or asked about the long-range effects that the bombing of Iraq's infrastructure would have on the civilian population. A report prepared in May 1991 by a Harvard study team predicted that 170,000 Iraqi children would die within the next year as a result of the effects of the Gulf crisis. One principal reason was that coalition bombing destroyed health and sanitation facilities, and agricultural production. A United Nations report said that thousands of Iraqis would die because of the "near-apocalyptic" conditions created by the bombing, and indicated that children and the elderly were especially at risk.

Evidence that while Defense Department personnel were complaining about the numbers of journalists from large media organizations who were sent to cover Operation Desert Shield, the Pentagon was providing transportation, escorts and special access to the battlefield for more than 150 reporters from smaller cities and towns so they could produce "Hi, Mom" stories about local troops stationed in Saudi Arabia. Most of the resulting coverage was highly supportive of the Defense Department's actions.

Evidence of a wider effort by the Bush administration to shape public opinion about the long-term effects of the Gulf War. A Jan. 25, 1991, Department of Energy memo ordered DOE contractors and personnel working in DOE facilities to "immediately discontinue any further discussion of war related research and issues with the media until further notice." [Emphasis is DOE's.]

The memo provided a script instructing personnel to tell reporters who wanted information on the environmental consequences of the war to state that "predictions remain speculative, and do not warrant any further comment at this time."

Evidence of a sophisticated public relations campaign by private organizations and foreign groups to build support for White House policies in the Gulf. In August 1990, Hill and Knowlton—a PR firm whose president and chief operating officer of public affairs, worldwide is Craig Fuller, Vice President Bush's chief of staff from

TV Was on the Spot

In the same way that high technology was used as never before on the battlefield, television news covered the Persian Gulf War with extraordinary immediacy.

CNN broadcast the war's beginning live from the US enemy's capital. Correspondents Peter Arnett, Bernard Shaw, and John Holliman described bombs and missiles striking within sight of their Baghdad hotel. Arnett stayed on in Baghdad throughout the war, broadcasting a range of stories while struggling against Iraqi censorship and worrying about his own safety.

Glimpses of the air war were popular on TV news. Video supplied by the US Defense Department gave an inside look at night-flight attacks over Iraq.

Canadian-born NBC News correspondent Arthur Kent achieved sudden celebrity as the "Scud Stud." In live broadcasts complete with rocket blasts, the handsome Kent reported nightly from Dhahran, Saudi Arabia, on Iraq's firing of Scud missiles and the allies' counterattacks.

1985 to 1989—was hired by representatives of the Kuwaiti government to help sell the American people on the need for U.S. military intervention. Hill and Knowlton's president and chief executive officer, USA, Robert Dilenschneider, said in a speech that the firm's job was "to build support behind the President." One way it did this, Dilenschneider said, was by providing the media, which were "controlled by the Department of Defense very effectively," with "the kind of information that would enable them to get their job done." Hill and Knowlton was paid more than $10 million for its efforts.

Indications that Bush administration officials were acting from political motivations when they decided to bar the media from Dover (Del.) Air Force Base during the arrival of caskets carrying troops killed in the Gulf War. During the 1989 U.S. invasion of Panama, two networks and CNN showed split-screen live coverage of President Bush joking with reporters before a press conference as the bodies of U.S. soldiers killed in the fighting arrived simultaneously at Dover. The president said at a later press conference that the coverage made him look callous, and had prompted negative letters to the White House.

Falklands War Provided Model of Press Control

The current system of media restrictions and information control is the latest refinement in a Pentagon and White House policy that has been evolving for more than 25 years.

The Vietnam War provided the impetus for the system's development. Many military officers believed that the United States lost the war because negative media coverage turned the American people against the conflict. In the late 1970s, Pentagon officials began searching for a new model for dealing with the press. They found one in Great Britain, where the Thatcher government had strictly controlled the media during the 1982 war with Argentina over the Falkland Islands. The fact that the Pentagon was interested in this model of press control had chilling overtones, because Great Britain still retains some of the press restrictions that led the Founding Fathers to adopt the First Amendment guarantee of press freedom.

One article written for a U.S. Naval War College publication outlined the lessons that the Pentagon could learn from the Falklands model. To maintain public support for a war, the article said, a government should sanitize the visual images of war; control media access to military theaters; censor information that could upset readers or viewers; and exclude journalists who would not write favorable stories. The Pentagon used all these techniques to one extent or another during subsequent wars.

Grenada Provided First Opportunity

The 1983 invasion of Grenada gave the Pentagon its first opportunity to try these news-management techniques. Pentagon personnel, with the knowledge and approval of the White House, barred journalists during the first two days of fighting. Reporters who tried to reach the island by boat were detained by U.S. forces and held incommunicado. Journalists who tried to fly in were "buzzed" by a Navy jet and turned back for fear of being shot down. Nearly all the news that the American people received during the first two days was from U.S. government sources. White House and Pentagon personnel reported that the conflict had been enormously successful and, in the words of Defense Secretary Caspar Weinberger, "extremely skillfully done."

In fact, the operation had been planned in great haste, and the first day's fighting had been a near-disaster for U.S. troops and a potential embarrassment for Pentagon leaders. For example, military officers did not know the location of many of the U.S. medical students they supposedly had come to save; U.S. troops were confused about the actual identity of the enemy and were supplied with tourist maps instead of strategic military maps; and more than a dozen innocent people were killed when U.S. forces accidentally bombed a mental hospital after mistaking it for a military installation.

In Panama Many Restrictions Politically Based

Evidence indicates that many media restrictions in Panama were politically based. For example, Defense Secretary Richard B. Cheney decided to make sure the DoD media pool would arrive too late to cover the early hours of Operation Just Cause after President Bush twice questioned pool members' abilities to maintain operational security. After the journalists arrived they were restricted to a U.S. base for several hours, listening to a lecture on Panamanian history and watching CNN television reports from the Pentagon to keep up on the progress of the war.

During the first several days, pool reporters were plagued by transportation and equipment shortages. Battlefield logistics were so confused that one plane carrying journalists was in danger of being shot down by U.S. forces.

During White House and Pentagon briefings about the invasion, officials misled reporters about U.S. casualties from friendly fire and low-altitude parachute jumps. Military officers deliberately concealed the fact that the controversial Stealth aircraft, which Cheney had praised for its "pinpoint accuracy" during the invasion, actually had missed both its targets by about 100 yards.

News Media Bear Some Responsibility

The media bear some of the responsibility for the increased restrictions on wartime coverage. Although journalists have complained for years about the restrictions, they have presented no effective opposition, and have frequently allowed themselves to be co-opted by the Pentagon and the White House.

For example, [although] the press complained about being confined to pools during the Gulf War, journalists fought among themselves for pool slots and turned in colleagues who tried to work outside the pool system. They presented no alternative that provided comprehensive answers for military officers' concerns about operational security and troop safety.

The media also failed to contribute sufficiently to public debate about the foreign policy issues that led to U.S. military involvement abroad. For example, before Operation Desert Shield began, [in August 1990,] few media reported regularly on the political, economic and historical factors that were influencing U.S. policy toward Iraq and Kuwait. Such stories, if run in a timely manner, might have had an important effect on public opinion and sparked a sharper congressional debate over U.S. military intervention.

Instead of developing a respectful but adversarial relationship with the Pentagon, many members of the press have become dependent on the military for visuals and information. For example, although reporters were physically prevented from watching and filming much of the fighting during the invasions of Grenada and Panama, the television networks showed hours of dramatic—and sometimes misleading—Defense Department footage. A similar situation developed in the Gulf, where the most exciting visuals during the air war were the Pentagon's carefully selected videos of precision-guided bombs demolishing their targets.

Some journalists believe that the lack of initiative displayed by many reporters covering the Gulf War was the media's single greatest failure, and will hurt future efforts to redefine the relationship between the Pentagon and the press.

The sad truth is that while reporters and editors complained about media restrictions, in the end many of them presented precisely the data and images that the White House and the Defense Department wanted the press to pass along to the American people.

Methodology

Research for this Center report has included examining dozens of books and articles by military officers and civilian Pentagon officials that discuss the relationship between the Defense Department and the press; analyzing thousands of pages of U.S. military documents; reviewing dozens of U.S. and British legal documents; reviewing hundreds of articles by journalists, academics and policy analysts in the United States and Great Britain, viewing hundreds of hours of television coverage and public affairs programs featuring speakers on all sides of the debate; studying transcripts of briefings and news conferences by White House, Pentagon and State Department officials; and interviewing dozens of people who served as military officers, Pentagon officials or journalists during World War II, Korea, Vietnam and the three operations in question. Material used in this study has been restricted as much as possible to primary documents and first-person accounts.

CHAPTER 3

Personal Narratives

A US Army Officer Sees the First Invaders Enter Kuwait City

Martin Stanton

The following viewpoint is unique. It is the account of the first American to witness Iraqi troops invading Kuwait—the action that led to the Persian Gulf War. Martin Stanton, a military adviser stationed in Saudi Arabia, had gone on leave, encouraged by his supervisors, for a long weekend in Kuwait City. In this account he tells of waking up in a Sheraton hotel to the sound of gunfire, seeing invading forces from his window, and calling in the initial reports. Stanton, a US Army major, was taken captive in Kuwait and held hostage by Iraq for four months.

Photo on previous page: A Kuwait City resident (center) embraces two US Marines after the allied liberation of the city on February 27, 1991. (**AFP**/**Getty Images.**)

SOURCE. Martin Stanton, *Road to Baghdad*. Copyright © 2003 by Martin Stanton. Used by permission of Presidio Press, an imprint of The Ballantine Publishing Group, a division of Random House, Inc. and Trident Media Group, LLC.

On 1 August [1990] I drove to Kuwait City—a long drive even at high speeds. Once I was past Jubayl, the empty desert seemed to stretch forever. The bleakness was punctuated only by the occasional gas station and the turnoff to the trans-Arabian pipeline (TAPLINE) road. I drove for hours listening to my tapes—Steely Dan, the Rolling Stones, and Enya. I recommend Enya, especially for long, lonely stretches of desert. The slow, haunting songs bring an almost otherworldly quality to desolate terrain.

At about two o'clock I reached Khafji, near the Saudi-Kuwaiti border, and had lunch. Khafji was the first real-sized town I had seen since leaving Jubayl. It was a pleasant little place with seaside villas and a small oil refinery. I was tired of driving and did not look forward to the usual border delays at customs that one normally encounters going from one country to another in the Middle East. I had been told it would take two to three hours to get through Kuwaiti customs, and I almost decided to cancel my plans to go there. The Khafji Beach Hotel was right in front of me, and the impulse to check in and go swimming was strong. However, I chided myself for laziness and drove on. Looking at the map, I could see that Kuwait City was only an hour or so from the border. Even if I was delayed at the border, I would still be at the hotel by about 6 P.M. With renewed resolve, I drove up to the border crossing.

The pessimists had been wrong. It took me only about an hour to get through customs, and all of the Kuwaiti border officials were courteous. I had a good conversation with a pleasant customs official in his mid-twenties about where to go in the city and some of the good places to eat and shop. He gave me a map and pointed out a few places. He apologized that he wouldn't be able to show me personally, but he gave me the phone number of his brother. I left feeling relatively positive about Kuwait.

Photo on following page: Iraqi tanks arrive in Kuwait City on August 2, 1990. (Time & Life Pictures/Getty Images.)

The drive to Kuwait City was a revelation. Whereas the roads in northern Saudi Arabia, although paved, were only two lanes wide, in Kuwait the road instantly went to a four-lane superhighway and I made excellent time. Everything I passed seemed newer and better constructed than in Saudi Arabia. It made sense: Kuwait was a richer country per capita than Saudi Arabia (or just about anyplace for that matter). That was evident from the spanking newness of much of the place. The city itself was very well laid out in a series of ring roads, and I easily found my way to the Sheraton, which was actually more than a mile from the main hotel district on the western side of town. It wasn't a particularly tall hotel (about twelve stories), but it was taller than most of the other buildings around it and offered a good view of the entire western side of town. I did not appreciate any of these characteristics until later, of course. At the time, in late afternoon on 1 August, I was just congratulating myself on having persevered and made the drive in one day. Now I wouldn't have to waste time going through the border in the morning. With a feeling of accomplishment, I drove into the Sheraton's parking lot.

> That's how the Iraqis first invaded Kuwait City—on buses, getting off like workers at the gates of a factory.

What a fool.

I checked into the Sheraton and went up to my room on the sixth floor. I had taken my binoculars and other items from the car because I didn't know whether Kuwait was as thief free as Saudi Arabia. After stowing my gear I went for a long walk around the city to stretch my legs. There were a lot of third country national (TCN) workers milling through the shops. In general it seemed like a normal evening in any of the Arab cities I had been in. A bit nicer though, and more modern. I found the gold souk, because I had resolved to get a present for Donna while I was in Kuwait. I ended up eating in a mediocre Chinese restaurant. After about four hours of rubbernecking around, I went back to my hotel room and took a shower. I went to bed at around 10:30. I would take a drive around town tomorrow and see the sights. I wondered vaguely what I would find, but I wasn't really excited about it. I expected only a mildly amusing weekend; that was all. Two weeks until I would see Donna again. Presently I fell asleep.

And while I was sleeping, the world changed.

Gunfire in Kuwait City

I awoke to gunfire about 4:15 on the morning of 2 August 1990. I was tired from my previous night's walk and had been in a very sound sleep, so it took a few moments for me to register what was happening. I lie there in bed and thought dreamily, *That sounds like shooting. . . . I wonder who could be shooting at this time of the morn—Shooting! Oh s---!* I dove out of bed and crawled to the sliding glass door to my balcony. Through the slats of the balcony railing I could see a lot of what was going on.

The first thing I saw of the invasion of Kuwait was that about a platoon of light infantry in uniforms I didn't recognize had secured the traffic circle to the southwest of the Sheraton. While I was watching, several buses, including one that looked like a Bluebird school bus, pulled up and started disgorging troops. That's how the Iraqis first invaded Kuwait City—on buses, getting off like workers at the gates of a factory. Several Toyota pickups with 14.5mm antiaircraft machine guns mounted on the back sped by. There was another flurry of firing from out of my field of vision, and all the soldiers I could see instantly took cover. A few of them started firing back down the street but were stopped by their officers after about a minute. The men stayed down for a few minutes, then gingerly picked themselves up and took up defensive positions around the traffic circle and the adjacent park, which was directly in front of the Sheraton. Soon another storm of small-arms fire erupted out of my field of vision to the south. But this time, although the troops had ducked down, as soon as they could see that the fire was not directed at them, they relaxed.

I was stunned. Clearly this was part of an invasion in strength. Most people had thought that Saddam Hussein [president of Iraq] had been just posturing. Rich Cassem [a major at the US Embassy in Saudi Arabia] had told me that, at the very most, Saddam might send troops into the northern oil fields of Kuwait, although he personally doubted that even this would happen. Apparently Saddam didn't know the script, because it looked as though he was going for the whole enchilada. Another triumph of U.S. intelligence.

Suddenly there was another burst of firing, and all the troops in the park went flat. A few of them started firing north into the parking lot that my car was in. Apparently a few armed Kuwaitis had fired at them from some government guard mount that they had overlooked, or maybe some of the local police were giving it their best effort. The Kuwaitis managed to keep the Iraqis in front of me pinned and crawling around for about five minutes. Then gradually the firing sputtered to a halt. I looked to see whether any of the Iraqis had been hit, but I couldn't tell. The fact that the city's lights continued to be on during all of this lent the firefight a surreal quality. I couldn't believe I was watching a real war.

Reporting to Headquarters

It occurred to me suddenly that I should tell someone about this. I crawled back to my nightstand and grabbed the phone. I looked up the U.S. embassy and tried to dial in. All the lines were busy. I then did an international direct dial (God bless calling cards). I got the OPM-SANG [Office of the Program Manager-Saudi Arabian National Guard] operator and demanded to be connected with

Brigadier General Taylor's house. He answered blearily but woke up fast when I informed him what was happening. He gave a low whistle when I described it to him, then asked me if I could positively identify Iraqis. I told him I could, because by then I could see the flags that some of their vehicles were flying. He told me to sit tight and keep reporting, then he hung up. In quick succession I called Colonel Noble and Rich Cassem. Noble was very quick on the uptake and asked only a few questions before going off to wake the rest of OPM-SANG's officers and men. Rich Cassem was incredulous. He reacted quickly, though, and told me to call him back in the defense attaché's office at the Riyadh [Saudi Arabia] embassy in about half an hour. Before he hung up, he hesitated and started to apologize for telling me that he hadn't thought the Iraqis would invade, but I cut him off. It wasn't his fault. He had simply believed the evaluations sent by intelligence people above him. The important thing was to stay in contact, so I told him to get to the embassy as fast as possible. Last I called Bob Quinn and told him to be prepared to help the Saudis roll the brigade, because I figured the call would come later that day (as it turned out, I was right). Bob took it like the pro he was, and I knew that my Vinnell team would be in there pitching. They were the least of my concerns. I told Bob that he had the reigns of the advisory effort until I got back or the army replaced me. He told me to take care of myself and not do anything stupid. I replied that I would be back as soon as I could and that I had already done something stupid: I had gone to Kuwait on pass. He laughed and wished me luck.

After hanging up, I felt desolate and alone. This was indeed a fine mess I had gotten myself into. I wondered how long the telephone would be in operation and resolved to call the Kuwait embassy again in a few minutes. Then I got the binoculars from my bag and crawled to the window for another look. More Iraqis had come into the circle and the park while I had been at the phone. They had set up two dismounted 106mm recoilless rifles, one apiece facing east and west on the main roads leading to the intersection. Each of the weapons had five ready rounds lying beside it; the crews were relaxed but ready at the weapons. There was firing in the town, but it was still out of my field of vision. More Toyota pickups with machine guns roared by. I could see what looked to be a battalion command group with officers and radiomen set up near a small, shaded structure in the park. I got my notebook and began to write down everything I observed and heard. I had the feeling it was going to be a very long day.

> Occasionally bullets smacked into the hotel front. I stayed down on my belly and was careful not to be seen.

Vehicles continued to go through the traffic circle. I looked for armor because I was certain that tanks would show up soon. The light forces that had infiltrated Kuwait City would have to be backed up by additional forces and armor. However, the only other Iraqi forces I saw for the next hour or so were additional school buses that brought in even more dismounted troops to be disgorged by the traffic circle and more Toyota pickups with heavy machine guns mounted. There were periodic bursts of firing in the city. Now that the sun had risen I could see dense black smoke coming from the south and west in several places. Periodically shots made the troops below me duck, and occasionally bullets smacked into the hotel front. I stayed down on my belly and was careful not to be seen, lest the nervous Iraqis below me think I was a sniper and begin firing at me. Enough bullets were hitting the hotel as it was.

The Start of Iraq's Invasion

After a few more minutes of looking out, I tried to get through to the Kuwait City U.S. embassy. The line was busy initially, but to my amazement on the second try the phone rang and was immediately answered. I quickly identified myself and told the person in the embassy where I was. I then tried to give them as complete a picture of what was going on in my field of vision as I could: the infantry reaching the traffic circle, the school buses and the Toyotas with machine guns, the 106mm recoilless rifles, and the incidents of firing I had seen. The man on the phone related to me that the embassy was not in a good position to see any of this because it was surrounded by high-rises on three sides and was near the water on the fourth. I told him that I had seen at least a brigade's worth of light infantry and that more troops were coming in all the time. He seemed taken aback at this but confirmed to me that the troops were indeed Iraqis and this was the invasion that Saddam Hussein had been threatening. I told him to look for me because I would try to make it to the embassy after dark (I had located it on my Kuwait City street map; it was about three kilometers from the Sheraton.) The man from the Kuwait embassy said that he understood but advised me to stay put for the time being because there was still a lot of shooting in the city.

> I realized that I had been foolish in my initial reaction to the invasion.

After hanging up, I realized that I had been foolish in my initial reaction to the invasion. God only knew how long the water and phone systems would last. The phone I couldn't do anything about; I would use it until the system was disabled. The water situation I could help. I immediately went into the bathroom, did a quick cleanup of the tub (hoping that the hotel staff had been thorough), then put in the stopper and filled the tub with water. I did the same with the sink. Then I took stock of the food in my room: a few cheese-and-cracker packets in my bag, my fruit bowl—courtesy of the hotel, two bottles of water, some packets of nuts in the little basket on the desk, and the mint from my pillow. That should sustain me for a couple of days. All in all my initial survival situation looked adequate. I went back to the window to take another look.

I got there just in time to see several helicopters fly past quickly, traveling north to Iraq. I didn't get a good look at the first two, but soon several others followed and I identified them as Russian MI-8 (HIP) troop carriers. Obviously they were traveling north after inserting troops somewhere in southern Kuwait. Several jets flew over at high altitude. I thought that this was another ill omen; clearly the Iraqis were using their air forces as well as ground forces in the invasion. Even at this early date, it was obvious that they were going for broke.

I tried to get through and update the Kuwait embassy on the helicopter movements I had just seen, but the lines were busy again. Then I remembered that I had promised to call Rich Cassem at the defense attaché's office in Riyadh. I was almost three hours late when I finally got through. I had to calm Rich and answer a few questions before I managed to finally convey to him that I was OK and still observing the situation. I gave him a brief update on everything I had seen and told him that in my opinion it was a full-scale invasion.

The War Is Fragments of Bravery, Death, and Confusion

Buzz Williams

On the ground during the Gulf War, US troops had to be ready for a surprise at any time. In the following viewpoint, a young Marine relates his experiences on two days of the war—February 24 and 28, 1991—in action to retake Kuwait from Iraqi forces. He drives an armored vehicle through minefields to attack enemy holdouts, some of them ready to fight and others eager to surrender. He also encounters a group of children—and a life-and-death illustration of political division in the Arab world. Reservist Buzz Williams rose to the role of company master gunner with six years of experience as a light armored vehicle crewman. After combat, he became a National Teacher of the Year and a public secondary school administrator in Maryland.

SOURCE. Buzz Williams, *Spare Parts: A Marine Reservist's Journey from Campus to Combat in 38 Days*. New York: Gotham Books, 2004. Copyright © 2004 by Buzz Williams. Used by permission of Gotham Books, an imprint of Penguin Group (USA) Inc.

The smog from the burning oil wells blanketed the sky, hanging just below black rain clouds, making even the night sight ineffective during midday. That left me driving with my head popped just above the safety of the armor, straining my eyes to avoid the hazards of the battlefield and keep us on the path into Kuwait City. When the rain clouds passed and the smog thinned out, we could see two hundred meters. Most of this day, though, we couldn't see our hand in front of our faces.

Dougherty and Sgt. Moss were talking constantly on the intercom, scanning for enemy tanks, bunkers, trenches, mines, and troops. Cpl. Shane stood up through the top hatch in back of the vehicle to cover our rear. Haley and our new scouts, Lance Cpl. Bennett and Lance Cpl. Wells, prepped their trench-clearing weapons in the rear of the LAV [light armored vehicle].

Although I wanted to be in the gunner's seat, Sgt. Moss convinced me to remain the driver. Regardless of the initial proficiency we had when we first picked up our LAVs, I now had logged the most time behind the wheel, and Dougherty behind the gun. Sgt. Moss explained that he needed the most experienced driver to keep us from hitting land mines, which threatened our lives as much as hostile fire.

That was true. The path through the breach was laced on both sides with engineer tape and tags marking mines. We rolled through the minefield breach for about an hour before entering the battlefield and opening our formation. Much of the Iraqi armor we encountered was in flames, already destroyed by the wave of M1 Abrams tanks that had rolled in ahead of us. We were to engage anything and everything that the tanks left behind. Dougherty pumped armor-piercing rounds into any tank that appeared intact, to be sure there were no Iraqis inside waiting to fire on us. It seemed more like target practice than combat.

Photo on previous page: Iraqi soldiers emerge from their protective bunkers to surrender to US soldiers in southeast Kuwait. (Associated Press.)

Action Breaks Out

The biggest threat during the first hours of the ground war was the hidden bunkers and trenches that harbored Iraqi infantrymen. Unlike the unknown danger of the stationary tanks the trenches were manned, and assumed to be hostile. Our first encounter with trench warfare was nothing like what we had practiced with Staff Sgt. Rodriguez. Not for us crewmen, anyway. Sgt. Moss was the first to identify the thin dark line, about a hundred meters to our front. We could see enemy soldiers moving in and around the trenches as we halted and called in our report. At first we followed procedure, and called to ask permission to engage the target. But there were so many targets, and so many requests to engage, the radio was jammed with traffic.

> The Iraqis told how they had wanted to surrender, but had feared being shot if they came out of hiding.

"... armed infantry in the open ..."

"... troops hiding in a bunker ..."

"... manned fighting holes to our front ..."

As the sound of LAVs started firing around us, Sgt. Moss took the initiative to issue his fire commands.

"Gunner! ... Troops in a trench! One hundred meters! On my position!"

Sgt. Moss, looking above the turret, reached down to his gun control and slewed the barrel to the general area of the trench. I tucked down into the hull and stared through the vision blocks.

Dougherty's voice followed. "Identified!"

"Fire!"

The first three-round burst thumped into the center of the trench. Three bright explosions lit the earth on impact, sending Iraqi soldiers running for their lives. Then Sgt. Moss ordered machine-gun fire.

"Gunner! Coax [denoting machine-gun rounds]! Troops in the open!" he said.

"Identified!" Dougherty called back.

"Fire!"

The spray zigzagged, blasting holes into the desert floor way short of the trenches. Dougherty adjusted and sprayed again, this time chasing the soldiers back into the trench to take cover. The main gun forced them out of the trench, and the machine gun forced them back in. Other crews in the company were experiencing the same frustration, but some had actually managed to take prisoners—and the prisoners talked. The Iraqis told how they had wanted to surrender, but had feared being shot if they came out of hiding. When we heard that over the radio, it changed our strategy completely. We still fired into the trenches with our main gun, but we did so at one end of the trench. Once the Iraqis exited the trench, we stopped firing, and sent our scouts to intercept them.

> After looking into their eyes it was difficult to hate them.

The strategy worked. Iraqi soldiers poured from their underground hiding places in droves. In a matter of hours our entire position was overrun with surrendering Iraqis. They walked right up to our vehicle with their hands on their heads, rifles slung upside down, and giant smiles on their faces. Haley, our lone Arab speaker, was invaluable in securing the prisoners. Many spoke English.

"We love George Bush!"

"USA! USA! USA!"

"America is great!"

When a wave of surrendering Iraqis moved past us, we fired on the trenches to clear them of any remaining Iraqis, and then moved on. God help the soldiers that had remained in hiding. Our firepower was devastating, and if they had not left when the others did, they would never get the chance.

I wanted them to live. With their famished frames, bloody feet, tattered uniforms, weathered skin, and pitiful expressions—they were pathetic. After looking into their eyes it was difficult to hate them. They were no longer evil, soulless killers. They were sons, and brothers, and husbands, and fathers. They didn't want to kill us any more than we wanted to kill them. . . .

A Day of Dealing with Children

They hid inside burned-out buildings, behind abandoned vehicles, and even underground, within giant craters carved by our B-52 bombers. They waited until our convoy was close, stopped, and vulnerable. Then they rushed from every direction, yelling, banging, and climbing onto our vehicles.

They were not enemy soldiers. They were children. Children desperate for water, food, attention, and assurance that the bad guys were gone.

We welcomed the rush. As soon as we stopped rolling, our hatches flew open and Marines poured out to assure them the good guys had arrived. As driver I was supposed to remain ready for the call to mount up and resume our road march. But the call to comfort the kids was too much.

"Sgt. Moss, can I go?" I asked.

"I wondered what took you so long to ask," he said. "Go ahead . . . but stay close!"

> We watched in horror as the car reversed, then accelerated again, intentionally aiming for the children.

The children swarmed to get my water, MREs [meals ready to eat], and sunflower seeds. The tall ones hugged my arms and the short ones clung to my legs. An older boy, maybe ten years old, rescued me from the siege. He organized the children into a group and distributed the water and food. They ripped the packages open and smashed the food into their faces like wild animals. My visit was brief.

"Back inside!" Sgt. Moss called. "Mount up!"

Before I left, the older boy handed me a paper Kuwaiti flag.

"Thank you. . . . Thank you, *jundee* (soldier). Come back. . . ."

I told him I would. It was a promise I couldn't keep.

They stood along the side of the road smiling, waving, and cheering as I climbed into the driver's hatch.

"Good luck!" I yelled to them.

My words were lost in the pandemonium that followed as a car broke through our column, headed for the children, still eating, drinking, and frolicking. They scattered just in time as the car raced over the spot where they'd been sitting. Had the car lost control?

No. It was no accident. We watched in horror as the car reversed, then accelerated again, intentionally aiming for the children. The older boy called for them to run for cover, guiding them through a break in the fence and over a guardrail separating the highway from their hiding places. One by one he pushed them through as the car circled around for a third pass. He barely made it through before it rammed the guardrail, the only thing stopping it from crushing him and the others. Then the car pulled back and, surprisingly, double-parked next to our column. Two civilian Arabs, carrying AK-47 rifles, got out and started yelling.

Haley interpreted. "They want our leader. They want to speak with the CO [commanding officer]."

The vehicle in front had already deployed its scouts, holding the Arabs at gunpoint until Capt. Cruz arrived.

After a brief exchange, Capt. Cruz shook hands with them, sent them on their way, and called all VCs [vehicle commanders] to his vehicle.

It wasn't what they did or said that earned the handshake. It was who they were. They were Kuwaitis—the *good* guys. The children were Palestinians—the *bad* guys.

Dougherty filled us in on the political implications over the intercom as we drove to our next position. He explained the historical hostility between the Palestinians and other established Arab groups. During peacetime Palestinians were outcasts among the people of Kuwaits, second-class citizens who were little better than slave laborers. As retribution many provided aid and comfort to the Iraqi invaders terrorizing the people of Kuwait, and [Palestinian leader] Yassir Arafat had spoken out in favor of Saddam Hussein's invasion. Although we had forced the Iraqi soldiers out of the city, many Palestinians remained behind. The conflict between returning Kuwaitis and traitorous Palestinians made the city a hotbed of civil unrest.

For Women in Combat, the Greatest Challenge Is Control

Rhonda Cornum, as told to Peter Copeland

A US flight surgeon, Major Rhonda Cornum was shot down on a rescue mission behind enemy lines on February 27, 1991. Though she survived, she was imprisoned with two broken arms, a smashed knee, and a bullet wound. In the following viewpoint, Cornum tells what she learned from that ordeal as well as other situations in the war. She became certain there is no reason to exclude women from combat, and that integrity, moral courage, and determination lead an individual to success. Rhonda Cornum is a medical doctor, pilot, paratrooper, wife, and mother, and holds a PhD from Cornell University in biochemistry. Peter Copeland is the Pentagon correspondent for Scripps Howard News Service. He spent three months with US troops in the Persian Gulf, reporting on soldiers' stories.

SOURCE. Rhonda Cornum, *She Went to War*. Copyright © 1992 by Rhonda Cornum. Used by permission of Presidio Press, an imprint of The Ballantine Publishing Group, a division of Random House, Inc.

Part of my responsibility is to understand what happened to me and help others learn from my experience. This is similar to what we always do in the army after an exercise or an operation: an after-action report of "lessons learned." I have some lessons that I learned from my six months in Saudi Arabia and my week as a prisoner of war in Iraq. The lessons are personal, professional, and I suppose political. People have asked how I am different or how the experience changed me, and I have to say that I don't think I've had any profound changes. Some people, when they have a brush with death, vow to change their lives or do things differently. I was a prisoner for only eight days, and the experience already feels like a brief chapter in my life. Instead, the lessons I learned confirmed many of the ideas I had before the war. One positive outcome was the opportunity to appreciate what I have, both in the personal sense of my family and in the broader sense of being an American. I also appreciate living in a small town. Our neighbors, our friends, took care of everything for us while we were gone, and they have been wonderful since we returned. We had no right to expect that. I have been amazed and very grateful.

Being a patient for the first time taught me some important lessons about medicine and being a doctor. Never before had I paid sufficient attention to the nursing staff, but nurses provided some of my most important care in Iraq and after I was freed. I will never again underestimate the contribution of nurses, physical therapists, and other staff. Some people suggested that I might become more sensitive to my patients as a result of being a patient myself. Maybe. I do know that I was the best source of information about what was wrong with me, not just because I am a doctor, but because I was the one with the broken bones. I also am now acutely aware of the feeling of helplessness that patients must endure. On the other hand, I probably will be even less tolerant of a patient who feels sorry for himself. I have never liked whining. Now I'm absolutely sure that whining does no good and might even slow the healing process.

My confidence level as a doctor received a boost from being in the desert, where I could not always rely on modern equipment or the second opinions of more senior doctors. If there was a problem, I was expected to solve it, and I did. I realize now that the training I have received in the army is excellent and truly prepared me for the real thing. I'm glad I went to the military medical school, where they stress the things we actually faced in the desert and the role of the "battalion surgeon" during war. I also saw many examples of truly selfless behavior among my colleagues. Teams of optometrists came to fit all our pilots who needed glasses with contact lenses so they could fly with the new gas masks, and teams from Medical Research and Development Command taught refresher courses on treating chemical casualties. The team lived and worked under very primitive conditions but never complained. Another example is a senior air force physician, the expert in night vision goggles, who gave classes all over the theater. He was tasked only with talking to air force pilots about the goggles, but he spoke to everyone from Riyadh to tents in the desert with the army's 8th Airborne Division, because he wanted all our pilots to have the best chance to make it back.

> "My confidence level as a doctor received a boost from being in the desert, where I could not always rely on modern equipment or the second opinions of more senior doctors."

Procedure Outweighs Medical Care

Were there problems? Of course. One night before the war a soldier ran up, breathless, to tell me a young man had fallen and was paralyzed. I ran down to the basement of the parking garage and found a group of people standing over a scared young soldier who said he could

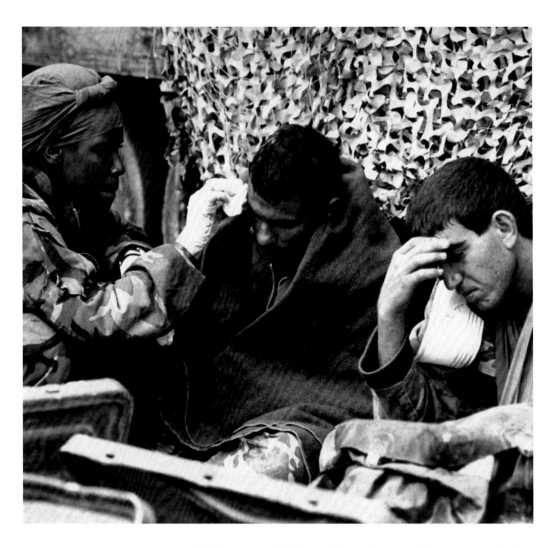

not feel or move his legs. One of my medics went to bring a pickup truck with a stretcher, and I knelt down to examine the soldier with another doctor who had arrived before me. We thought he might have fractured his lower spine when he fell on a large ridge of concrete. I held the soldier's hand and reassured him, but I knew he would have to be airlifted to a hospital.

We put him on a spine board and a stretcher, drove him out of the garage onto the flight line, and loaded him onto a waiting helicopter. The pilot asked me where to go, and I told him the Air Transportable Hospital in Dhahran. After a twenty-minute flight, the patient was in the emergency room, where he was X-rayed and seen by the orthopedic surgeon. He was terrified, afraid he would never walk again, and he asked me to stay with him at the hospital while he was evaluated. I spent the night and got a ride the next day back to King Fahd.

When I arrived, I learned the brigade surgeon was looking for me. He and the division surgeon were upset that we had taken the patient to an air force hospital instead of to the army's 28th Combat Support Hospital, which was undeniably closer. I explained that I had visited the army's hospital just hours before the soldier fell, and at that time there was no working generator, and thus no X-ray capability. Since the first thing this soldier needed was films, I couldn't see any reason to go there. Apparently that didn't matter. I received a letter shortly after from the division surgeon saying that I had done the wrong thing. The officers in my chain of command defended my decision, but I was angry that some people seemed more concerned with procedure than with appropriate medical care.

A Shared Military Mission

Despite occasional irritation with the system, my experiences were overwhelmingly positive, and have made me more committed than ever to military medicine. As stated in the motto, the goal of military medicine is to "conserve the fighting strength" of the armed forces. Over the years, I have seen the positive impact "medics" can have on morale and readiness, but it was dramatic during the deployment to the Middle East. Maj. Jonathan Letterman, a surgeon in the Union Army, said it best more than a hundred years ago:

> A corps of medical officers was not established solely for the purpose of attending the wounded and the sick. . . .

The labors of medical officers cover a more extended field. The leading idea, which should constantly be kept in view, is to strengthen the hand of the Commanding General.

With the daily pressure to provide care for a huge population of dependents and retirees, I am afraid that we sometimes lose sight of that goal. Another goal often forgotten is that military doctors also are soldiers who must be ready for combat. Some people think there is a contradiction between being a doctor and being a soldier, but I certainly don't. As a professional officer, I took an oath to defend the Constitution and to guide my actions with the principles of "duty, honor, country."

> Some people think there is a contradiction between being a doctor and being a soldier, but I certainly don't.

As a physician, I took an oath to do what is best for my patients to the best of my ability. I haven't found any ethical dilemmas arising from adhering to both. I identify myself as a doctor and as a soldier, and I value both professions equally. Some people think the Hippocratic oath tells us, "Do no harm," but in fact we promise to do no harm to our patients. Nowhere does the oath say a doctor takes on the entire world as patients.

Military medicine does have its share of "Hawkeyes," folks who don't take the military seriously, although they are very serious about medicine. Apart from embarrassing other officers, they do fine in a peacetime environment. When we are not in the field, we basically practice medicine like civilians, especially in the big medical centers. During wartime, however, the commander must have confidence in the medical officer in his unit and on his staff. He needs to know that the physician has the same professional standards, ethics, and experiences as other officers. He needs to know the "Doc" will give him good advice based on the mission of the unit. If the physician is so ignorant of the military that he (or she) doesn't understand the mission, he can't possibly give good advice and will likely not have the plans, equipment, and supplies necessary to provide the best possible care for the soldiers. In my view, like the Union Army's Major Letterman's, that is the real reason for having military physicians.

Another lesson I brought home from the Gulf is that men and women can work well together. Saudi Arabia was a harsh reminder that America is not a Moslem society where women and men must be strictly segregated. Men and women like each other's company, both at home and in the workplace, so I think having men and women in the army actually is a plus. The war did not change the attitudes of the men I know, but then they already had worked with women and know it's possible, even desirable. The war might have changed the attitudes of some men who had never served with women for long periods under difficult circumstances. Part of the problem is generational: older people in the military have a harder time with men and women serving together. The young generations are used to playing soccer together, studying together, and being friends, not just boyfriends and girlfriends. For many young people, working together in the army is the natural order of things.

Women Belong in the Military

The war dramatized the fact that the role of women in the military already has changed. We are no longer nurses and typists serving in rear areas—there were nearly forty-one thousand women in the Gulf working as doctors, nurses, pilots, mechanics, truck drivers, cooks, clerks, intelligence officers, communication experts, and in a host of other specialties. There were women in every part of the theater, from the headquarters of General [H. Norman] Schwarzkopf to a few women in the foxholes in Iraq and Kuwait. In my opinion, the war showed that America is ready for army women, all of whom volunteered, to serve throughout the army and not be excluded from combat jobs. Parents back home didn't miss their sons less than their daughters, and kids didn't miss their dads more or less than their moms.

Many people have asked if my opinion about "women in combat" has changed after my experience. In fact, I think exactly what I have always thought, that everyone should be allowed to compete for all available jobs, regardless of race or gender. There is no question that the "average" woman is not as tall, heavy, or strong as the "average" man: we don't need a congressional committee to tell us that. But what does that mean? I'd say it means that if the job requires someone to be tall, heavy, and strong, then fewer women will be competitive than men. But at least let them compete. Who cares what percentage qualifies?—just pick the best. On the other hand, there are many jobs for which height, weight, and strength are irrelevant. We should let all people compete for those jobs as well.

> I don't think 'combat exclusion'—the rule that keeps women out of combat jobs—helps anyone.

The qualities that are most important in all military jobs—things like integrity, moral courage, and determination—have nothing to do with gender. Everybody in the army—whether he or she enlisted, went to a military academy or ROTC [Reserve Officers' Training Corps] or received a direct commission—all volunteered to serve. No one has been drafted or otherwise coerced. I believe the military pays members for two things: the jobs they do daily and the willingness to risk their lives if called to war. Personally, I don't think "combat exclusion"—the rule that keeps women out of combat jobs—helps anyone. If I were a male soldier, I would resent women making the same money and holding the same rank but not being responsible for taking the same risks. On the other hand, combat experience is not only an important factor for advancement (as it should be) but ultimately is the reason for having the military. As a female soldier, I would resent being excluded. We preach "equal opportunity" everywhere. I believe we should also be preaching "equal responsibility."

One area of responsibility for everyone, including military people, is having children. Like joining the military, having children is a decision people make, not something that occurs randomly like lightning or cancer. If an individual, male or female, feels that being a parent is not compatible with a military profession, that person certainly has the option of postponing children or changing careers. But I don't believe that the people who feel that parenting and a military life are incompatible should determine everyone else's career or parenting decisions. I am extremely happy with my family and both my professions, the military and medicine. Neither my family nor I feel that my career and family life have been at all incompatible. I am inspired by the fact that [daughter] Regan and [husband] Kory love me and are proud of me not only as a mother and a wife, but also as a doctor and a soldier.

> Your captors can torture you and even kill you, but you still have control as long as you can think.

What about all that famous male bonding? Well, when a unit contains only men, you certainly get male bonding. When there are women present, you get male and female bonding. I just call it unit bonding, and it does occur. Whether a unit "bonds" or not is based on many things: the circumstances, the leadership, the threat, and the makeup of the unit's members. When we were in the desert, people got along well and bonded just fine. I've been to war with a combat unit, and the men in our unit did not try to protect the women any more or less than the rest of their comrades. . . .

Responsibility and Control

My commanders agreed that the presence of a woman did not hurt our unit's performance. In my Officer Evaluation Report for the period from August 13, 1990, through February 27, 1991, the day we were shot down, Lieutenant Colonel Bryan wrote about me:

> Outstanding performance in combat. Rhonda Cornum is the finest aviation medical officer in the Army. She is a tough, no-nonsense officer who has demonstrated magnificent technical skill combined with outstanding leadership. Rhonda had the most profound impact on the combat effectiveness of my battalion. Rhonda Cornum makes things happen. People follow her anywhere. She goes where the soldiers need her. A true ultimate warrior.

Colonel Garrett, the commander of the 101st Aviation Brigade and my senior rater, added: "Rhonda Cornum is chock full of the right stuff."

Being a prisoner of war [POW] is the ultimate loss of control, especially for a POW with two broken arms. The best analogy I can think of is rape, and both experiences have the potential to be devastating. Being a POW is the rape of your entire life. But what I learned in those Iraqi bunkers and prison cells is that the experience doesn't have to be devastating, that it depends on you. Other POWs, and most recently the hostages released from Lebanon, have found the same thing: you can *give* up control of your mind, but no one can take it away from you. Your captors can torture you and even kill you, but you still have control as long as you can think. I remember wondering if my body would ever be strong again, if my arms would ever heal, if I would ever be able to run again. I wasn't sure how I would adjust to being slower or permanently disabled, but I convinced myself that as long as my brain was working, I would be fine. I think the idea was best expressed by David Jacobsen, who was held hostage in Lebanon: "As long as you have your brain, your mind, you are free."

I am very, very blessed to be here, free, today.

The Lives of Iraqi Teenagers Changed Drastically Because of the War

Nadje Al-Ali and Yasmin Hussein

A decade after the Persian Gulf War ended, teenagers in Iraq lived with anxiety about even their basic needs, according to the following viewpoint by Nadje Al-Ali and Yasmin Hussein. Through in-depth interviews with young people, the authors found typical days were in fact unpredictable and filled with struggles for survival. The most normal aspiration was to leave Iraq as soon as possible. Education remained important, and many were hopeful, but the Iraqi teenagers were living in isolation. Al-Ali and Hussein worked as members of Act Together, a British-based group of Iraqi and non-Iraqi women. They researched and wrote this viewpoint for the Institute of Arab and Islamic Studies at the University of Exeter.

SOURCE. Nadje Al-Ali and Yasmin Hussein, "Between Dreams and Sanctions: Teenage Lives in Iraq," Act Together: Women's Action for Iraq website, 2001. Copyright © 2001. Reproduced by permission of Professor Nadje Al-Ali.

Only two years after the end of the Iran-Iraq war, [president of Iraq Saddam] Hussein ordered Iraqi troops to invade Kuwait in August 1990. Economic sanctions were imposed a few days after the invasion. The Gulf War of 1991 forced Iraq out of Kuwait. But it also resulted in the death of many Iraqis and the devastation of the Iraqi infrastructure. Up to the day of writing this [in 2001], continued economic sanctions and sporadic bombing of Iraq have had detrimental effects on both social and economic conditions in Iraq.

Due to the very particular circumstances in contemporary [Iraq], it is very difficult to describe a 'typical day' for an Iraqi teenager. In the past, young Iraqis would go to school in the mornings, return for lunch between 2 and 4 o'clock, have their main meal with their family, maybe nap for an hour or two, especially in the summer months, do their homework and study and then enjoy themselves with friends and family. In the evenings, when everyday life was still relatively ordinary and calm, teenagers would go out and walk the streets in groups, have ice-creams or *shawarma* sandwiches, play games with their friends from the same neighbourhood and visit their numerous cousins, watch TV and listen to the latest hits.

These days, everyday lives are characterised by unpredictability and struggles for survival. Leila, a 16-year-old teenager, expressed sentiments that many young Iraqis feel:

> I hope to finish my education and become a civil engineer, and would like to feel that I am a significant part of society. I would like to be economically independent, but share the responsibility for raising a future family together with a man whom I will respect and love as much as he would respect and love me. I think this dream is a basic thing for many people, but it seems so hard to actually make true. Although I have strong faith in my

A boy fishes on the banks of the Shatt al-Arab river in Basra, Iraq, before the Gulf War. During the 1970s and 1980s, Iraqi teens and adults experienced a high quality of life and rising wealth. (Getty Images.)

heart and believe that I shall make it one day, I cannot deny that I fear the unexpected things that could change everything. Our lives in Iraq are so unpredictable, especially the economic situation, which has a decisive impact on all aspects of our lives. So my mood is swinging all the time: Sometimes I feel optimistic, but most of the time it is hard to ignore the reality of our lives. This is why I often get depressed. Now, for example, I am very disappointed by the results of my high school exams. I really believe that I have done all my best to pass this level with a satisfactory result, but that was obviously not good enough. And now I have to repeat the whole year in order to get better grades. I truly believe that the examinations of the next year will be even harder than this year . . . (Leila, 16 years old)

Leila's passionate account of her dreams and fears quite vividly illustrates the fact that teenagers in Iraq have a lot in common with teenagers in other countries all over the world: they worry about their grades in school, have ambitions what their future careers are concerned, and they think about love. Teenagers everywhere dream about having enough money and many hope for a future spouse that will care for and respect them. And who has not met an adolescent who is experiencing and displaying mood swings—being very happy one moment and extremely down and depressed the next?

Yet, despite the commonalities with teenagers in other parts of the world, most notably the Middle East, Leila and her peers in Iraq experience daily hardships and obstacles to fulfil their dreams that are unique to their specific surroundings. The devastation of two wars (Iran-Iraq war 1980–1988 & Gulf War 1991) and ongoing economic sanctions have left their country in a desperate situation.

Leila's worries about the 'unpredictability' of life in Iraq and 'the unexpected things that could change everything' typify the fears and anxieties of a whole generation that grew up in times of extreme upheaval related to war, ongoing military threats, an oppressive regime and economic sanctions that reduce everyday lives to a continuous struggle for survival.

Post-War Sanctions Affect Everything

This chapter reveals both: the universal concerns, aspirations and anxieties of teenagers who happen to live in

Iraq, as well as the extreme conditions, difficulties and suffering that are unique to Iraq and the lives of its adolescent population. At the heart of these contributions are the voices of several teenagers who were specifically interviewed for this volume. They were asked questions related to their everyday lives, their aspirations and worries. There are several reasons why the researchers opted for a mainly qualitative approach to the exploration of teenage lives in Iraq: First of all, it is very difficult to obtain reliable statistical information in the Middle East in general and Iraq, in particular. More significantly, the available statistics tend to conceal rather than reveal the actual experiences, attitudes and life strategies of a group of people that has been silenced from within and without.

Through extensive in-depth conversations and interviews with a group of teenagers between the ages of twelve and sixteen, the authors of this chapter were able to get a sense of the present living conditions shaping their lives and restricting their choices. Yet, they got an insight into the emotional landscapes of young Iraqis, their self-awareness and attitudes to 'the outside world'. The recorded interviews touch on a broad range of issues varying from social change and transformations, problems with education, economic hardships, relationships with families and friends, gender relations and identity questions. Yet, an underlying theme is the awareness that many of the numerous difficulties facing young Iraqis today stem from an imposed sanctions regime that has not only devastated the economy but has also affected the social and cultural fabric of Iraqi society.

References to 'rapid social changes' and transformations of 'normal lives' are common in the accounts of teenagers. Despite indisputable political repression in the 1970s and 1980s, the majority of the Iraqi population enjoyed high living standards in the context of an economic boom and rapid development, which were a result of the rise of oil prices and the government's developmental policies. Although signs of deterioration of living standards started to become evident during the years of the Iran-Iraq war (1980–1988), there seemed to be the prevailing belief that the situation would revert to the better once the war stopped. And while many families lost sons, brothers, fathers, friends and neighbours during this time, life in the cities appeared relatively 'normal', with women notably playing a very significant role in public life.

> "Adolescent Iraqis invariably have vivid memories of the Gulf War and many spoke about ongoing nightmares, a sense of anxiety and a great sensitivity to certain noises."

Today's teenagers (age group 12–16) were born during these war years, when the Iraqi government encouraged everyone to fulfil 'their duties' as citizens. While men were drafted in large numbers to the military, women were strongly encouraged to 'produce' numerous children. Only two 'peaceful' years were followed by the invasion of Kuwait (August 1990) and the Gulf War (January–March 1991). The latter was particularly traumatising for children, as night after night of heavy bombing disrupted not only their sleep and family lives, but left many in deep shock and fear. Adolescent Iraqis invariably have vivid memories of the Gulf War and many spoke about ongoing nightmares, a sense of anxiety and a great sensitivity to certain noises that could only remotely be mistaken for bombs. Unlike other war-torn countries, like Bosnia-Herzegovina, for example, 'post-traumatic stress syndrome' is not a recognised medical condition in Iraq. And even if acknowledged, lack of resources and expertise make systematic treatment impossible.

While the memories related to the war in 1991 as well as political oppression by the Iraqi government represent crucial elements in the pool of experiences that constitute 'the past' of today's teenagers, it is the comprehensive sanctions regime, in place since August 1990, that presents the most decisive factor in shaping the everyday living conditions, options and restrictions of Iraqi teenagers. Continuously high rates of child mortality (about 4000–5000 per month), rampant malnutrition, increased rates of leukaemia, various other forms of cancer, epidemic diseases and birth deformities are amongst the most obvious 'side effects' of the sanctions regime.

> Family relationships have been strained by envy and competition in the struggle for survival.

The fear of disease and death are a real and a steady companion while growing up these days. The massive deterioration in basic infrastructure (water, sanitation, sewage, electricity) has severely reduced the life quality of Iraqi families, who often have to get through the day without water and electricity. Everyday lives have changed not only with respect to a drastic deterioration of economic conditions and basic infrastructure, but the social and cultural fabric of Iraqi society has also been affected.

Many Wish Strongly to Leave

Alongside the drastic changes related to everyday lives, the intellectual and cultural isolation that accompanies ongoing economic sanctions affect teenagers in various ways. Some feel resentful and angry by an 'international community' that does not seem to care about the plight of ordinary Iraqis and seems to punish them for the actions of a government they did not choose. Others do distinguish between certain western governments, and the people and culture of these countries. In light of difficult, if not impossible, access to alternative media and education other than government propaganda, teenagers often do not have the analytical tools and background information that the previous generations had. This, paradoxically, amongst other factors has strengthened the regime of Saddam Hussein. Yet, a surprising number of teenagers do not only blame the outside world, but also their own government for the current situation. And many have just one wish: to leave their homeland as soon as possible and start a new life somewhere else. Hazim, a fourteen-year old boy, whose mother recently died, often dreams of leaving, but finds strength in his faith:

> Sometimes I do think that our lives have become harder than before. But I have to remember that God is with us, and that we need to be strong to manage everyday life. But sometimes I really think that it would be better to escape to another place where life is easier and much happier.
>
> [*Where do you think such life exists?*]
>
> Everywhere in the world, apart from Iraq and maybe some places in Africa. I often give myself time to dream of living in another part of the world, and imagine myself living differently than this miserable life. But I quickly remember that God has chosen this kind of life for me and I think it is some sort of test of my faith in God.

Traditionally, Iraqi families—like most families within the region—played a significant part in young people's lives. Children and teenagers were not only brought up by their parents, but also by their elder siblings and members of the extended family, like grandparents, aunts and uncles. Families tended to be large and provided not only material but also emotional support for teenagers. Because of the size of most families, gatherings were generally not only an affair for adults, but children of all ages and teenagers were always present.

Although Iraqi families used to be very closely knit and supportive of each other, family relationships have been strained by envy and competition in the struggle for survival. More than a decade of economic sanctions have exhausted the Iraqi economy and most people living inside Iraq. In the past, teenagers grew up in the midst of their extended families, often spending time and sleeping over at houses of their grandparents, uncles and aunts. These days, nuclear families have become much more significant in a context where everyone has to think about himself or herself and those closest to them first.

1979   Saddam Hussein becomes president of Iraq.

1980–1988   Iran-Iraq War takes place.

1989   George H.W. Bush becomes president of the United States.

1990   July 17: Saddam accuses Kuwait of stealing oil from areas claimed by Iraq.

July 31: Iraqi and Kuwaiti delegations meet in Jidda, Saudi Arabia, but fail to resolve their differences.

August 1–2: Iraqi military units invade Kuwait and occupy the country.

August 2: The United Nations (UN) Security Council demands Iraq withdraw from Kuwait.

August 3: A strong majority of nations in the Arab League Council votes that Iraq should leave Kuwait.

August 7–8: Bush demands that Iraq withdraw, and orders US military units dispatched to defend Saudi Arabia and "other friends in the Persian Gulf." The troop movement is known as Operation Desert Shield.

August 28: Saddam declares that Kuwait is now the nineteenth province of Iraq.

November: Half a million Iraqi troops are in position to defend Iraq and captive Kuwait.

November 29: The UN Security Council authorizes "all necessary means" to force Iraqi troops out of Kuwait by January 15, 1991.

1991   January: The United States assembles an international coalition force in the Persian Gulf region at least as large as Iraq's.

January 9: Meeting for six hours in Geneva, Switzerland, US secretary of state James Baker and Iraqi foreign minister Tariq Aziz fail to reach an agreement.

January 12: The US Congress authorizes use of offensive force in the Persian Gulf.

January 17: US Army helicopters lead the first strike of Operation Desert Storm into Iraq. (Bush's live TV announcement that the war had begun came just after 9 P.M. Eastern Standard Time on January 16, but with the eight-hour time-zone difference it was already the next day in Iraq.)

January 18: Iraq fires eight Scud missiles into Israel in the first of a series of such attacks on that country and Saudi Arabia.

January 27: The US-led coalition achieves total dominance in the air.

February 21–22: Iraq begins destroying oil wells in Kuwait.

February 24–25: Desert Storm's ground offensive begins in full. The coalition wins major battles along the Iraqi border, and its airborne troops strike deep inside Iraq.

February 26–28: Coalition troops win large-scale battles in several crucial areas and liberate Kuwait.

February 28: With the Iraqi army in total retreat, Bush orders the US-led coalition to stop shooting and offers Iraq a cease-fire. Coalition troops do not attempt to capture Baghdad.

March 1–2: Some Iraqi units fire on US troops, provoking a battle in the area of the oil fields along the Kuwait-Iraq border.

March 3: Iraqi military officers admit defeat to the US commanding general, H. Norman Schwarzkopf.

March 4–5: Forty-five allied prisoners of war are released.

April: The United States begins to institute no-fly zones in the Gulf, declaring large parts of the sky off-limits to Iraqi military planes.

April 3: Iraq agrees to a UN demand to get rid of its nuclear, chemical, and biological weapons as well as all missiles with a range greater than 150 kilometers.

June 26: US warships fire twenty-four missiles at the Iraqi intelligence headquarters in Baghdad in retaliation for a plot to assassinate Bush during a visit to Kuwait.

2001 George W. Bush becomes president of the United States.

2003 March 20: After more than a decade of rising tensions and charges that Saddam was again amassing weapons of mass destruction, a US-led air strike begins a new war with Iraq.

FOR FURTHER READING

Books

Association of the U.S. Army, *Special Report: The U.S. Army in Operation Desert Storm: An Overview*. Arlington, VA: AUSA Institute of Land Warfare, 1991.

Rick Atkinson, *Crusade: The Untold Story of the Persian Gulf War*. Boston: Houghton Mifflin, 1993.

Amatzia Baram, *Iraq's Road to War*. New York: St. Martin's Press, 1993.

James Blackwell, *Thunder in the Desert*. New York: Bantam Books, 1991.

Richard Engel, *A Fist in the Hornet's Nest: On the Ground in Baghdad Before, During & After the War*. New York: Hyperion, 2004.

Norman Friedman, *Desert Victory: The War for Kuwait*. Annapolis: U.S. Naval Institute Press, 1991.

Avigdor Haselkorn, *The Continuing Storm: Iraq, Poisonous Weapons, and Deterrence*. New Haven and London: Yale University Press, 1999.

Molly Moore, *A Woman at War: Storming Kuwait with the U.S. Marines*. New York: Charles Scribner's Sons, 1993.

Michael A. Palmer, *Guardians of the Gulf: A History of America's Expanding Role in the Persian Gulf: 1883–1992*. New York: Free Press, 1992.

H. Norman Schwarzkopf and Peter Petre, *It Doesn't Take a Hero: The Autobiography of General H. Norman Schwarzkopf*. New York: Bantam Books, 1992.

Richard Swain, *Lucky War: The Third Army in Desert Storm*. Fort Leavenworth, KS: U.S. Army Command and General Staff Press, 1997.

Anthony Swofford, *Jarhead: A Marine's Chronicle of the Gulf War and Other Battles*. New York: Scribner, 2003.

U.S. News & World Report, *Triumph Without Victory: The History of the Persian Gulf War*. New York: Times Books, 1993.

Bob Woodward, *The Commanders*. New York: Simon and Schuster, 1991.

Periodicals

Stephen A. Bourque, "Correcting Myths about the Persian Gulf War: The Last Stand of the Tawakalna," *Middle East Journal*, vol. 51, no. 4, 1997.

Robert Brenner, "Why Bush Went to War," *New Left Review*, no. 185, February 1, 1991.

Angelo M. Codevilla, "Magnificent, But Was It War?" *Commentary*, April 1992.

John K. Cooley, "Pre-War Gulf Diplomacy," *Survival*, March/April 1991.

Trevor N. Dupuy, "How the War Was Won," *National Review*, vol. 45, no. 5, April 1, 1991.

"Armchair Generalship: The Gulf War Revisited," *Economist*, vol. 3, no. 23, May 2, 1992.

Tom Engelhardt, "The Gulf War as Total Television," *Nation*, May 11, 1992.

William F. Fore, "Analyzing the Military-News Complex," *Christian Century*, April 17, 1991.

Glenn Frankel, "Iraq: Despotism Amid the Ruins," *Washington Post*, April 9, 1991.

Peter S. Kindsvatter, "VII Corps in the Gulf War: Deployment and Preparation for Desert Storm," *Military Review*, vol. 72, 1992.

Edward N. Krapels, "The Commanding Heights: International Oil in a Changing World," *International Affairs*, vol. 69, January 1993.

Charles Krauthammer, "The Unipolar Moment," *Foreign Affairs*, vol. 70, no. 1, 1991.

Chris Kutschra, "Kuwait: Called to Account," *Middle East*, no. 217, November 1992.

Jim Naureckas, "Gulf War Coverage: The Worst Censorship Was at Home," *Extra!*, vol. 4, no. 3, May 1991.

Harold H. Saunders, "Political Settlement and the Gulf Crisis," *Mediterranean Quarterly*, Spring 1991.

Yezid Sayigh, "Why Iraq Could Not Win," *Middle East International*, no. 395, March 8, 1991.

Norman Schreiber, "Management Under Fire: The Paradigm of Desert Storm," *Management Review*, vol. 80, no. 11, November 1991.

Joseph M. Siracusa, "George Bush and the Gulf War: A Just War or Just Another War?" *Social Alternatives*, vol. 10, no. 2, July 1991.

Abdullah Toukan, "The Gulf War and the Environment: The Need for a Treaty Prohibiting Ecological Destruction as a Weapon of War," *Fletcher Forum*, Summer 1991.

Lonnie Valentine, "The Gulf Wars Syndrome," *Peace Review: A Journal of Social Justice*, vol. 19, no. 4, 2007.

Websites

CBC Digital Archives, The 1991 Gulf War (http://archives.cbc.ca/war_conflict/1991_gulf_war/topics/593/). This website was compiled by the Canadian Broadcasting System and contains thirty-two television and six radio broadcasts on the Gulf War.

Frontline, The Gulf War (http://www.pbs.org/wgbh/pages/frontline/gulf/). A website with content from a PBS program first broadcast January 9, 1996, provides analysis and commentary on the 1990–91 war. It features interviews with key political and military figures of the war, including Colin Powell, Norman Schwarzkopf, and Margaret Thatcher. It also presents the stories of US and British soldiers taken prisoner during the war.

INDEX

A

Abbas, Tumah, 33, 58–59

Abdulla, Abdulkhaleq, 68–78

Act Together, 194

Air control and warning aircraft (AWACS), 20

Air Transportable Hospital, 187

Al-Ali, Nadje, 194–202

Al-Nasser, Gamal Abd, 34

Al-Rasheed Hotel, 50, 56, 59

Al-Razzaz, Mu'nis, 101

Albright, David, 32

Algeria, 18

Amaduja, Iraq, 117

Amyotrophic lateral sclerosis (ALS), 146

Anthrax vaccine, 146, 148

Apache attack helicopter (Boeing AH-64), 19, 26

Aquinas, Thomas, 81

Arab-Israeli wars, 38

Arafat, Yassir, 182

Argentina, 160

Arnett, Peter, 158

Atkinson, Rick, 5

Augustine (Saint), 81, 85

Aziz, Tariq, 35, 54, 58, 103

B

Ba'th Party, 58, 137

Baghdad, Iraq

Baghdad meeting, 139

Gulf War destruction, 12, 13, 20, 128, 129

New Year celebration 1991, 49–59

prisons, 57

See also Iraq

Bahrain, 16

Baker, James A. III, 54, 58, 62, 103

Bard, Mitchell, 99–108

Barrow, Robert H., 86

Bessmertnykh, Aleksandr A., 111

Birth defects, 200

Black market, 57, 59

Blackhawk helicopter, 106

Boeing AH-64. *See* Apache attack helicopter

Bohemian Grove, 128

Boomer, Walter, 66–67

Bosnia-Herzegovina, 199

Brain cancer, 146

Bulletin of the Atomic Scientists, 86

Bush, George H.W.

advisers, 137

aggressiveness, 96

announcement of US military build-up, 37, 104

criticism of Bush war policies, 128, 130, 135, 140, 141

deception about Gulf War, 151–163

defense of decisions in Gulf War, 126

Executive Orders, 44–45

freezing Iraq and Kuwait assets, 44–45

Geneva meeting and, 35
Hussein and, 41, 62
National Security Directive 45, 42–48
new world order and, 64, 65, 72
photographs, *44*, *61*, *153*
public opinion ratings, 152
response to Iraqi invasion of Kuwait,
  16–18
US support of UN resolutions and,
  43–44
war announcement, 60–67
Bush, George W., 5

C

Cassem, Rich, 170–171, 174
Center for Public Integrity, 152
Chediac, Joyce, 132
Chemical agent resistant coating (CARC),
  146
Chemical and biological weapons, 21, 37,
  63, 100, 148
Cheney, Richard B. (Dick), 106, 161
Children (Iraqi)
  malnutrition, 128, 133, 133–135
  mortality rates, 200
  traumatization, 199
  UNICEF (United Nations Children's
    Fund), 134
  US Marine assistance, 180–182
Chronic fatigue syndrome, 146, 149
Civilian casualties, 6, 94–96, *95*
Clark, Ramsey, 125–135
Clausewitz, Carl Philipp Gottlieb von, 89
CNN, 51, 158, 159, 161
Cobra helicopter, 106
Cohen, Saul B., 116–124
Collateral damage, 94
Colonialism, 72

Combat exclusion rule, 190–191
Copeland, Peter, 183–193
Cordesman, Anthony H., 13–27
Cornum, Rhonda, 183–193

D

DaPonte, Beth, 130
Dehydration, 131
Desalination plants, 123
Desert Storm. *See* Gulf War
Dilenschneider, Robert, 159
Double effect, 94
Dover Air Force Base (Delaware), 159
Dunlap, Robert, 156

E

Egypt, 18, 25, 34, 121, 139
Electric power, 133, 200
Ellerkmann, Richard, 58
Embargo on Iraq
  black market, 57, 59
  Bush and, 63
  effect on teenagers, 195–200
  export embargo, 18–19, 50, 55
  food shortages, 128, 133
  inflation and, 59
  justification for war and, 96
  luxury goods and, *52*
  malnutrition and, 128, 133, 133–135
  medicine shortages, 128
  oil embargo, 47–48
  post-war sanction, 197–200
  smuggling and, 59
  social effects, 198–199, 201–202
Emergency Economic Powers Act, 44
European Union, 123–124
Exit strategy, 4, 32

Exocet missiles, 112

F

Fahd, King of Saudi Arabia, *138*, 139, 187
Falklands War, 159–160
Fatah Revolutionary Council, 101
Fatigue, 146, 149
Fibromyalgia, 146
First Amendment, 152, 160
Fitzwater, Marlin, 132
Food (Iraq)
   destruction of agricultural production, 157
   embargo on food imports, 128, 133
   food storage, 53
   malnutrition, 128, 133, 133–135
   rationing, 55
   restaurant closures, 56
   shortages, 55, 127–128
"Force multipliers," 110
Fragmentation bombs, 132
France, 16–17, 25, 31
Freedman, Lawrence, 28–41
Fuel-air explosives, 132
Fuller, Craig, 158

G

General Dynamics, 106
Geneva Convention of 1949, 128
Geneva talks, 35, 54, 58, 62
Germany, 58, 118
Geyer, Alan, 92–98
Ghareeb, Edmund, 136–142
Glaspie, April, 32
Goldwater–Nichols Defense
   Reorganization Act, 113

Great Britain, 15–17, 25, 163
Green, Barbara G., 92–98
Greenpeace, 130
Grenada, 135, 152, 154, 160–162
Gulf Cooperation Council (GCC), 16, 47–48
Gulf War
   advantages of coalition forces, 112–115
   Arab countries' attempt at preventing, 139–142
   beginning, 19
   Bush administration deceptions, 151–163
   Bush announcement, 60–67
   casualties, 6, 94–96, *95*, 110–111, 124, 126, 157
   causes, 13–27
   coalition land forces, 22–26
   coalition losses, 110–111
   criticism of US policies, 92–98
   destruction in Iraq, *12*, *27*, *83*, 157
   exit strategy, 32
   genocide by US and, 125
   geographical considerations, 37–38
   goals, 6, 63, 65–66, 71–72, 85, 155–159
   Gulf region instability, 68–78
   highways of death, 132
   Iraqi losses, 110–111, 124
   Iraqi soldier surrender, 179–180
   jihad, 35, 137
   as justifiable, 80–91
   map, *76*
   Middle East power structure and, 116–124
   moral issues, 93
   neurotoxic exposures, 144–145
   photographs, *12*, *164*, *167*, *176*
   post-war sickness of US troops, 143–150
   prisoners, 179, 183, 192
   private video firms, 156–157

propaganda and, 49, 96, 156–159
public support, *79*, 97
reparation claims, 107–108
training US military, 185
women and, 183–193
See also Just war tradition; Medical
   care; specific countries
Gulf War Syndrome, 143–150

H

Hamdoon, Nizar, 51

Hamza, Khidhir, 32

Harvard International Study Team, 133,
   157

Have Nap air-launched missiles, 105

Hill and Knowlton, 158–159

Hippocratic oath, 188

Holliman, John, 158

Hostages, 19, 31, 50, 165, 192–193

Huddleston, Hollywood, 66–67

Husayn, King of Jordan, 139–140, 142

Hussein, Saddam
   Arab-Israeli conference, 30–31
   Bush and, 41, 62
   Coalition forces and, 65
   geographical considerations, 37–38
   Iraq's debt and, 13
   Israel's enemy, 99–100
   new world order and, 77–78
   New Year celebration 1991, 51
   nuclear weapon development, 32
   photograph, *73*
   Powell and, 4
   psychological weaponry, 40–41
   public opinion, 170
   removal from power, 5–6, 117
   war preparations, 28–41, 64
   See also Iraq

Hussein, Yasmin, 194–202

I

International Energy Agency (IEA), 45

Iran, 20, 69, 72, 75, 118

Iran-Iraq war
   air power and, 38–39
   cause for Gulf War, 13
   costs, 69
   economic effect in Iraq, 199
   length, 69, 197
   military operations, 36–37

Iraq
   aircraft in Iran, 20
   assets in US frozen, 44–45
   barricades in Kuwait, 35–37
   Baath (Ba'th) Party, 58, 137
   casualties in Gulf War, 110–111, 124,
      126
   clemency for Iraq after Gulf War, 5–6
   economic rehabilitation, 120
   excuses for invasion of Kuwait, 14–16
   families, 201–202
   foreign debt, 13, 14, 15, 75
   frozen assets in US, 18, 44–45
   Gulf War destruction, *12*, *27*, *83*, 157,
      195
   hostages, 19, 31
   infant mortality, 134
   inflation, 59
   Jordan and, 101
   Kurds, 100–101, 117–119, 124
   looting of Kuwait, 54–55, 117
   military forces, 25, 26, *29*, 33, 38–40, 54
   naval blockade, 19
   oil exports, 141
   oil quotas, 14
   post-Gulf War, 133–135, 194–202
   Shia Muslims, 117, 119, 124
   terrorist training bases, 101

UN inspection teams, 6
weapons, 6, 15, 62–63, 100–104, 112, 120
See also Baghdad, Iraq; Embargo on Iraq; Food; Gulf War; Hussein, Saddam; Water
Iraqi Air Force, 100
Iraqi Museum, 55–56
Israel
    Gulf War and, 21, 34, 99–108
    Hussein and, 99–100
    IDF (Israel Defense Force), 105
    Iraqi nuclear reactor destruction, 39, 103
    reparation claims, 107–108
    Scud missiles and, 104, 131
    Six Day War, 122
    Soviet immigration, 123
    weapons development and, 105–106
Israeli Aircraft Industries, 105–106

J

Jacobsen, David, 193
Janier, André, 50
Japan, 18
Jidda (Saudi Arabia) meeting, 139–141
Jihad, 35, 137
Johnson, James Turner, 80–91
Joint Chiefs of Staff, 4
Jones, Jackie, 66–67
Jordan, 18, 101, 139
Just war tradition
    criteria, 81
    hope of success, 89–90
    just cause, 81–82
    moral questions, 93
    peace restoration, 86–87
    proportionality of good and evil, 87–89

right authority, 83–84
right intention, 84–86, 94
war as last resort, 90–91, 96–97
See also Gulf War

K

Karbala, Iraq, 53
Karsh, Efraim, 28–41
Kelly, Thomas, 156
Kendall, J.P., 66–67
Kent, Arthur, 158
Khadduri, Majid, 136–142
Khalaf, Salah, 56
Khan, Abdul Qadeer, 32
Korean War, 19, 163
Kurds, 100–101, 117–119, 124
Kuwait
    embargo, 47–48
    financial aid to Iraq, 14
    frozen assets, 45
    Fund for the Future, 16
    goal of Gulf War, 6
    looting by Iraqis, 54–55, 117
    oil quotas, 14
    Palestinians and, 181–182
    photograph of Iraqi invasion, *167*
    post-Gulf War, 120–121
    propaganda and, 159
    request for US protection, 46
    responsibility for Gulf War, 75, 77
    witness to invasion of, 165–174
    US Embassy, 172–173

L

LAV (light armored vehicle), 177, 178
Lebanon, 18, 30, 192, 193
Lehman, John, 128

Lennon, John, 57
Letter, Jonathan, 187–188
Libya, 18, 135

M

Malnutrition, 128, 133, 133–135
Mansour Melia Hotel, 50
Mauritania, 18
McPeak, Merril A., 155–156
Media restrictions, 151–163
Medical care
    Air Transportable Hospital, 187
    battalion surgeon, 183–193
    coalition bombing and, 157
    goal of military medicine, 187
    malnutrition, 128, 133–135
    medicine shortages in Iraq, 59, 128,
      131–132
    post traumatic stress disorder, 144, 199
    pyridostigmine bromide (PB), 144–145,
      147–150
    US troop sickness post-Gulf War,
      143–150
    wounded soldiers, 184–185
Memory problems, 149
MEW, 130
Minefields, 177
Mirage aircraft, 39, 112
Moore, Molly, 7
Mosul, Iraq, 117
Mubarak, Husni, *138*, 139, 140
Multinational Force for Saudi Arabia
  (MNFSA), 46–47
Multinational Force to Enforce Sanctions
  (MNFES), 46–48
Multiple chemical sensitivity, 146
Muscle/joint pain, 149

N

Najaf, Iraq, 53
National Emergencies Act, 44
National Security Directive 45, 42–48
Naval blockade, 19
NBC News, 158
Neal, Richard, 130
Netherlands Embassy in Iraq, 58
Neurological problems, 149
Neurotoxic exposures, 144–145
New world order, 64, 65, 72, 77–78
New York Times, 86
NFL Films, 156
Nidal, Abu, 101
North Atlantic Treaty Organization
  (NATO), 18
Nuclear Non-Proliferation Treaty, 103
Nuclear energy, 39
Nuclear weapons, 32, 63, 100, 103–104

O

Oil
    cause for Gulf War, 104, 137
    conflict and, 70, 74
    embargo, 47–48
    Iraq's oil exports, 141
    oil pipelines, 123
    oil war, 74
    oil well fires, 145, 177
    prices, 40, 72, 74, 82
    reserves, 56, 74
    US imports, 45
Oman, 16
One-man/one-party/one-family regimes,
  69, 75, 78
Operation Desert Shield, 4–5
Operation Just Cause, 161

OPM-SANG (Office of the Program Manager-Saudi Arabian National Guard), 170–171

OXFAM, 134

P

Pagonis, William G., 128

Paine, Thomas, 66

Palestine, 100, 122, 142, 181–182

Palestine Liberation Organization (PLO), 56, 101, 122

Panama, 135, 152, 154, 159, 161–162

Patriot missiles, 21, 105, 155

Peddling Peril: How the Secret Nuclear Trade Arms America's Enemies (Albright), 32

Pentagon, 124, 128, 154–156

People (magazine), 128

Perry, William J., 109–115

Personal stories
    battalion surgeon, 183–193
    Iraqi teenagers, 194–202
    US Army officer witness to invasion of Kuwait, 165–174
    US Marine in ground war, 175–182

Pesticides, 145, 147–150

Pioneer pilotless drones, 105

PLO (Palestine Liberation Organization), 18, 122

Post-traumatic stress disorder, 144, 199

Powell, Colin
    career highlights, 4
    counting enemy dead and, 128
    leadership style, 4, 113
    Operation Desert Shield and, 4–5
    Secretary of State, 5, 43–44
    Vietnam War and, 4

Powell Doctrine, 4

Propaganda, 49, 96

Psychological weaponry, 40–41

Pyridostigmine bromide (PB), 144–145, *145*, 147–150

Q

Qatar, 16

Quantum Diversified, 156–157

Quinn, Bob, 171

R

Reconciliation, 93

Repentance, 93

Republican Guard, 25, 26, 38, 51

Research Advisory Committee on Gulf War Veterans' Illnesses, 143–150

Riyadh, Saudi Arabia, 171, 174

ROTC (Reserve Officers' Training Corps), 190

Rumalia oil field, 14, *17*

S

Sa'd, Shaykh, 139

Saddam's Bombmaker (Hamza), 32

Safe Haven Camps, 117–118

Sanctions *See* Embargo

Sarin (chemical weapon), 148

Saudi Arabia
    Bush and, 18
    Hussein and, 16
    Iraqi missile attacks, 21
    Kuwait invasion by Iraq and, 15, 170–171, 174
    leadership, 139
    OPM-SANG, 170–171
    post-Gulf War, 121
    request for US protection, 46

troops in Gulf War, 25
  UN coalition forces and, 14
Saunders, Harold, 96–97
Schroeder, Pat, 86
Schwartzkopf, Norman, 24, 63, 113, 128, 152, 189
Sciolino, Elaine, 49–59
Scud missiles, 21, 99, 104–108, 131
"Scud Stud," 158
Shah of Iran, 69, 72, 75
Shanshal, Abd al-Jabbar Khalil, 33
Sharkley, Jacqueline, 151–163
Shaw, Bernard, 158
Shia Muslims, 117, 119, 124
Six Day War, 122
Smuggling, 59, 100
Soviet Union
  breakup, 7
  Gulf War and, 14, 18
  immigration to Israel, 123
  Middle East influence, 121, 123
  UN Resolution support, 31
  US ally, 14
Stanton, Martin, 165–174
Stealth aircraft, 14, 19–20, 114, 161
Sudan, 18
"Supergun," 101
Syria, 6, 18, 25, 30

T

Talfah, Dnan Khairallah, 33
Tanks, 14, *167*, 177
Telephone service, 57, 170–171, 173
Thatcher, Margaret, 137, 159–160
Theft, 55, 168
This Morning (TV news program), 126

Time (magazine), 133
Tomahawk cruise missiles, *102*, 103, 106
Transportation, 133
Tumors, 149
Turkey, 117
Turkish Empire, 15

U

UN. *See* United Nations (UN)
Under Fire: U.S. Military Restriction on the Media from Granada to the Persian Gulf (Center for Public Integrity), 152
UNICEF (United Nations Children's Fund), 134
Union Army of US, 187–188
United Arab Emirates, 16
United Nations Participation Act, 44
United Nations (UN)
  coalition forces in Gulf War, 14
  deadline, 58
  economic sanctions on Iraq, 6
  Hussein removal from power, 6
  Iraq embargo, 19, 140
  just war tradition and, 81–82
  membership, 62
  peacekeeping forces, 117
  reparation claims for Gulf War and, 107–108
  Resolution 238, 122
  Resolution 242, 122
  Resolution 660, 18–19, 43, 46, 48
  Resolution 661, 45, 46, 48
  Resolution 662, 43
  Resolution 678, 31, 84
US Army, 165–174
US Census Bureau, 130
US Central Command, 156
US Code, title 3 section 301, 44

US Constitution, 84, 188
US Department of Defense, 114, 147, 152–156, 158, 161, 163
US Department of Energy, 157
US Marines, 25, 175–182
US Naval War College, 160
US Secretary of Defense, 48
US Secretary of Energy, 45
US Secretary of State
    Baker, 54, 62
    freezing Iraq and Kuwait assets in US, 45
    petroleum reserves, 45
    Powell, 5, 43–44
US Secretary of the Treasury, 45
USA Today (newspaper), 86
Uranium, 103, 146, 148

V

Vaccines, 145
Vietnam War
    ill-prepared troops and, 113
    Iraqi perception of US involvement, 18, 32–34, 39
    negative media coverage, 159–160
    Powell and, 4
    report on media coverage of Gulf War and, 163

W

Walker, Harold, 58
War Powers Act, 84
Washington Post, 5
Water (Iraq)
    contamination, 128, 131
    quality of life and, 200
    shortages, 127–128, 133–134, 173

storage, 53
Weaponry
    air control and warning aircraft (AWACS), 20
    Apache attack helicopters, 19–20
    arms trade in Middle East, 123–124
    Blackhawk helicopter, 106
    chemical and biological weapons, 21, 37, 63, 100, 148
    Cobra helicopter, 106
    Exocet missiles, 112
    "force multipliers," 110
    fragmentation bombs, 132
    fuel-air explosives, 132
    Have Nap air-launched missiles, 105
    Iraq weaponry, 6, 15, 62–63, 100–104, 112, 120
    Israeli weapons development, 105
    Mirage aircraft, 112
    nuclear weapons, 32, 63, 100, 103–104
    Patriot missiles, 105, 155
    precision-guided weaponry misconceptions, 126–127
    psychological weaponry, 40–41
    Scud missiles, 21, 99, 104, 106, 107
    smuggling, 100
    stealth aircraft, 14, 19–20, 114, 161
    "supergun," 101
    tank fire-control systems, 14
    Tomahawk cruise missiles, *102*, 103, 106
Weinberger, Caspar, 127, 160
West Bank annexation, 122
White House, 154, 158
Williams, Buzz, 175–182
Wilson, Joseph C. IV, 50, 57–58
Woman at War (Moore), 7
Women, 56, 86, *129*, 183–193, *186*
World War I, 15
World War II, 163

Y

Yemen, 18, 121

Z

Zakho, Iraq, 117